Liberating the Na
History Curricul

Josna Pankhania

Routledge
Taylor & Francis Group

First published in 1994
by Falmer Press

This edition first published in 2018 by Routledge
2 Park Square, Milton Park, Abingdon, Oxon OX14 4RN

and by Routledge
711 Third Avenue, New York, NY 10017

Routledge is an imprint of the Taylor & Francis Group, an informa business

© 1994 Pankhania

The right of Josna Pankhania to be identified as author of this work has been asserted by her in accordance with sections 77 and 78 of the Copyright, Designs and Patents Act 1988.

Publisher's Note
The publisher has gone to great lengths to ensure the quality of this reprint but points out that some imperfections in the original copies may be apparent.

Disclaimer
The publisher has made every effort to trace copyright holders and welcomes correspondence from those they have been unable to contact.

A Library of Congress record exists under ISBN: 0750702087

ISBN: 978-1-138-57306-2 (hbk)
ISBN: 978-0-203-70167-6 (ebk)
ISBN: 978-1-138-57320-8 (pbk)

Liberating the National History Curriculum

Once there were bards who sang the songs which kept the listeners in touch with their past. They reminded them of the heroes who once walked among them and whose legacy provided a sense of shared greatness and national identity. Later, the bards became historians and history teachers and English history became a glorious roll call of those who had gone out and created an Empire and, at the same time, spread education and enlightenment. But recent doubts have raised questions about partiality and perhaps there were losses suffered by the Empire's people. Perhaps "their" heritage should be "our" heritage and therefore a fit subject for history to deal with.

Originally published in 1994, this book argues that the curriculum can be legitimately used to teach students the history of oppressed groups. It is important to note that Pankhania manages to do this, not in a divisive spirit but with the intent to seek unity for the future by understanding and accepting the positive and negative aspects of a collective past.

Liberating the National History Curriculum

DEDICATION

To John, Rohan and Mira

Liberating the National History Curriculum

Josna Pankhania

 Falmer Press

Taylor & Francis
London . Washington, DC

UK   The Falmer Press, 4 John St, London WC1N 2ET
USA   The Falmer Press, Taylor & Francis Inc., 1900 Frost Road, Suite 101, Bristol, PA 19007

First published 1994

A catalogue record of this publication is available from the British Library

ISBN 0 7507 0208 7 cased
ISBN 0 7507 0209 5 paperback

Library of Congress Cataloging-in-Publication Data are available on request

Jacket design by Caroline Archer

Typeset in 10/12 pt Times by
Graphicraft Typesetters Ltd., Hong Kong

Contents

List of Figures

Acknowledgments

I remember the time when I thought that I could not write English properly and my husband John Macdonald persuaded me otherwise. I would like to thank him for all his love and support and always rejoicing in my roots and heritage. I would also like to thank Rohan, my son, and Mira, my daughter, for showing me the wonder of this world.

Professor Gajendra Verma has been a constant source of support and encouragement, his experience and useful insights have been invaluable in the writing of this book; Godfrey Brandt of the Commonwealth Institute has been more helpful than I had any right to hope. I am grateful to both of them.

This book owes much to Maniben Pankhania, my mother, and Harjibhai Pankhania, my father, whose struggles and respect for the Indian culture have been a source of inspiration for me. I regret that my father, my brother Shantilal and my sister Pravina, who lived such short lives, will not be able to read the book. My brother Rajnikant and sister Harsa have contributed towards this book in ways they probably do not realise; I thank them for this.

I am grateful to Sarah Macdonald, my mother-in-law, who offered me support not only when I was writing this book but during the years that we were together before she died. She was one of the finest feminists that I have ever known.

I would like to thank Robert Ballard and Jonathan Reddiford who contributed to this book with helpful advice and comments.

I would also like to thank Jan Miller for doing the illustrations and maps for this book and for offering her skills and time so generously. Anna Lucia Cuevas did the illustration of the First Nation People of North America and for this I thank her too. I am grateful to the Association of Gaza Artists for their permission through War on Want and UNAIS to reproduce their drawing on page 139. I would also like to thank the India Office Library for the permission to reproduce the photographs on pages 111 and 135, and the Mary Evans Picture Library for the permission to reproduce the illustration on page 120. Finally, I would like to thank Survival International for their permission to reproduce their photographs on pages 130 and 131.

It has to be said that during the long time that it has taken to write this book, the understanding and patient support of my editor, Malcolm Clarkson, has been most important to me, and for this I thank him.

Foreword

Once there were bards. Poets and musicians, they sang the songs which kept the listeners in touch with their past. They reminded them of the heroes, demi-gods and gods who once walked among them and whose legacy to their descendants was a sense of shared greatness and a national identity.

Later the bards became historians and history teachers. Their function was much the same. English history was a glorious roll-call of heroes who had gone out and created an empire whilst, at the same time, spreading education and enlightenment.

More recently there were doubts. Perhaps history should be less partial. Perhaps it should have something to say about the losses which the Empire's peoples suffered as well as the gains from which they benefited. Perhaps 'their' heritage ought, in some sense to be 'our' heritage and therefore a fit subject for history to deal with.

At first sight, the National Curriculum appeared to dismiss any such notions. It aimed to offer a limited kind of history in which consideration of issues, such as the development of race, gender and class inequalities, were to be ignored or positively discouraged.

This book clearly demonstrates that the National History Curriculum is actually a broad outline of subject areas and argues that teachers retain the freedom to use teaching materials of their own choice. *Liberating the National History Curriculum* is about exactly that: how the curriculum can be legitimately used to teach students the history of oppressed groups. It is important to add that this is done, not in a divisive spirit but with an intent to seek unity for the future by understanding and accepting the positive and negative aspects of a collective past. I commend it to all teachers of history.

Gajendra K Verma
Professor of Education and
Dean, Research and Graduate School
University of Manchester.

Introduction

After three centuries of exporting African slaves to the Americas, Britain created a new system of slavery known as the 'indenture labour' system. This new form of slavery lasted for ninety years, and it allowed the British to recruit thousands of Indians to go and work on Britain's former slave plantations and other colonies for a pittance. Although the indenture labour system was legally terminated in 1920, the recruitment of Indian labourers by the British colonials continued for several decades. Often only the men went, with hopes of a better future for themselves and their loved ones. One of these men was my grandfather who went in search of employment from Gujerat to East Africa. After some years, he was followed by his son, my father, who also left his small family behind him in India. A decade later, my mother and two brothers joined my father. My two sisters and I were born in Kenya.

A child of the Indian diaspora, I grew up in Africa and I went to a school that the British had generously built and where I was taught many things. In my history lessons, I learned the names of the great European explorers who sailed in their magnificent ships all over the world. I learned the dates when different parts of Africa were 'discovered'. This education taught me that civilization did not exist in Africa until the Africans were enlightened by the Europeans. I also learned the names of the European geniuses who made great contributions to the advancement of their countries through the machines that they invented, for example, the Spinning Jenny, the steam engine, the radio, etc. This education taught me that Africa and India were undeveloped because their people lacked intelligence and creativity.

I remember speaking in English in my African school, for in many ways my friends and I were discouraged from speaking in an African or an Indian language. I remember learning about 'Humpty Dumpty', 'Old Mother Hubbard', 'Ba Ba Black Sheep', and later about *Alice in Wonderland*, *The Wizard of Oz*, *Robinson Crusoe* and *The Adventures of the Secret Seven*. This education taught me that Africa and India have no children's literature worth pursuing in schools. At home when my mother sang Indian songs to me, I felt embarrassed and wished my parents would speak to me in English. I hid my mother tongue in a world that was increasingly portrayed as ugly.

When I came to England at the age of twelve with my family, I was awarded a place at a prestigious Grammar School; my education in East Africa had served me well. My new school friends asked me if in Africa we lived in houses, wore grass skirts, had proper schools, cooked our food. My education continued . . .

In history in my English school, I learned the names of all the great kings and queens of Britain and the dates of when they reigned. I learned the dates of when all the great wars were won. In English Literature, Shakespeare was not new to me. I studied Dickens and Hardy too. For Religious Instruction I remember gaining numerous 'merits' for the verses I learned by heart from Matthew, Mark, Luke and John and it was not long before the hymns that we sang daily in Assembly were engrained on my Hindu mind. In music I did not quite manage to grasp the violin, but I learned to recognize various symphonies of Beethoven and Sonatas of Mozart; I passed in music too. In this way I learned about how Europe is advanced and why Britain is Great. The high grades that I received at school almost made me an expert, and I began to take it for granted that Europeans are a superior race and that black people have a great deal to learn from them. As I grew older, I realized that in my experience of racism in education, I was not alone.

My school was neither a place where my Indian identity was nurtured nor a source of knowledge about the history of my people. My teachers did not offer me information or encourage me to develop skills to analyse the nature and causes of inequalities in society. In many ways, I was taught to accept that black people are somewhat 'backward', that the rich people of this world have gained their just rewards because of their intelligence and their own hard work and labour, that most poor people are lazy and ignorant, that the primary role of women in society is to care for their families, and that men are best equipped to deal with the world outside the home.

As an adult I have learned that there are numerous explanations for why there are inequalities in society. Chapter 1 will examine some of these theories with the conviction that a coherent theoretical perspective is essential, not only to enable us to understand social inequalities, but also to work effectively towards justice. Many theories appear plausible on the surface, but the question that will be asked is, do these theories inform us about the historical development of social inequalities and challenge exploitation or do they simply justify oppression? Religious, biological, cultural, functionalist and feminist theories will be examined. It will be argued that in order to understand inequalities in society, we need to examine the history of how some people have become rich and others have been made poor. This requires a study of social, economic and political relationships through history between the powerful and oppressed. Making sense of inequalities in society and its institutions, such as the education system, is then possible.

Chapter 2 focuses on one group of people who experience inequality in this society — young black people in the British education system. (Black people here refers to all people who experience European racism. The term black stems from the colonized peoples' own frame of reference which differs from white Eurocentric descriptions of colonized peoples as 'negroes', 'coolies', 'coloureds', 'ethnic minorities', 'wogs', etc. Black is therefore a political term to identify the existence of the oppression and resistance of black people.) The chapter argues that to understand the present position of black students in British schools, it is necessary to examine the relationship that the British state has had with black people through history. Certain questions are central to such an examination. When, why and how did the contact between Britain and black people first begin? How did this contact develop? The study of the historical relationship between Britain and impoverished black women, men and children illustrates that a significant part of Britain's contact with black people had been based on slavery, indentured labour and colonialism. Without understanding this historical relationship, it is not possible to make sense of the present position of black people in British society and in Britain's education and other institutions.

The denial of the history and the identity of black people was an important strategy used by the British and other Europeans to enslave and colonize black people for, by portraying people as less than human, it is easier to treat them as work animals. Today, the majority of the British people believe that they live in a free, egalitarian and democratic country. Indeed, over the last three decades, various governments have requested special committees to examine the needs of black students and to formulate policies for improving the position of young black people in the education system. Chapter 3 argues that although a great deal of concern has been expressed about the position of black students in British schools, the major multi-racial education policies do not urge schools to nurture the identity of black students and to equip white students to live responsibly in Britain's multi-racial society by learning about the history of black people.

The National History Curriculum (England and Wales) (DES, 1991), following the footsteps of thirty years of multi-racial education policies, does not encourage the teaching of black history in schools. Chapter 4 argues that the National History Curriculum (England) rarely acknowledges the historical relationship between Britain and black people. The great contribution of black people towards the building of Britain, black people's experiences of oppression and black people's struggles for justice and liberation are either ignored or skimmed over. Not only does the National History Curriculum disregard the historical experience of the black peoples of the British colonies, it also minimizes the contribution of the British women and working-class men and children. By disregarding the history of British racism, sexism and class oppression, the National History Curriculum attempts to teach students a limited history, a history that does not threaten the British social order with its unequal race, gender and class relations.

If the aim of history is to help students to make sense of the past in order to understand the present and to respond to the future constructively, then the history that they are taught should not be based primarily on the selected glories of the past. Making sense of the present from half truths about the past is not possible. With a distorted understanding about the present, it is not possible to participate fully in society.

Fortunately, at present, the British State's National History Curriculum (England and Wales) is a broad outline of subject areas, and teachers have the freedom to use teaching materials of their own choice. Thus teachers who are interested in teaching, not simply about Britain's greatness through history but also about how Britain became 'Great', can do so with imagination and careful planning. Chapter 4 also illustrates how teachers can liberate the National History Curriculum and encourage students not only to learn about the history of racism but also about the history of sexism and class oppression. In this way the history of black people is not compartmentalized but is situated within the context of a people's history. The aim of liberating the National History Curriculum is not to be divisive but to seek a unity for the future by understanding and accepting the positive and the negative of our collective past.

As a thread of black and white working-class people's history is woven into the National Curriculum, the brutal oppression of the British state in relation to its people and its subjects becomes apparent and the myth of Britain being a 'land of hope and glory' crumbles rapidly. For this reason, some white teachers may prefer not to challenge the History Curriculum or to question the traditional British and Eurocentric ideas perpetuated within the school system. This book argues that unless we understand and come to terms with the beauty and the warts of our collective history, we will not be able to make sense of the present and respond constructively to the future. The history of all people after all has oppressive as well as liberating elements. The beauty of Britain's history is the struggle of its people and the people of its empire for justice; the warts of the British history are the dehumanizing forces with which Britain has ruled over 'its' people and 'subjects'.

Chapter 5 offers suggestions for lesson plans and attainment targets which aim to weave an anti-racist thread into the National Curriculum. The lesson plan outlines have been drawn up with an assumption that history teaching should encourage students to develop historical skill within the context of investigating the history of how people lived in the past and related to each other. The aim of the lesson plans is therefore to offer students an opportunity to develop historical skills of evaluation, abstraction, analysis, synthesis, empathy and communication while exploring the social, economic and political relationships between groups of people through history. In the process of exploring the past, it is hoped that students will learn to locate information from a range of sources, recognize bias, omissions, and irrelevances, situate the evidence within a historical context and communicate their findings in a variety of creative reconstructions, such as plays, exhibitions, projects, etc. Most importantly, it is hoped that students will gain some understanding of the dialectical nature of history, that history is not a study of isolated, unrelated incidents of the past but is a critical exploration of the historical social, economic and political forces that have impacted upon groups of people in the past and continue to do so today.

An imaginative adaptation of the National History Curriculum can be an opportunity to challenge the British state's plans to teach the next generation a limited history which does not threaten the unequal race, class and gender relations in our society. Teachers may wish to flow with the historic tide of domination or they may choose to offer students some insight into the historical forces of oppression and liberation. The choice is each individual teacher's.

Chapter 1

Making Sense of Inequalities in Society

Why is it that there are some groups of people in society that are rich and others are poor? How is it that some groups of children 'succeed' at school and others 'underachieve'? Is it because God wanted it thus? Is it because some people are born with greater talent than others? Is it because some people work harder than others?

A coherent theoretical perspective is essential, not only to understand the unequal position held by the oppressed in our society but also to live consciously in the present and to work effectively towards justice. In order to arrive at a broad theoretical understanding, general social theories as well as specific education theories on inequality will be examined in this chapter. Some theories appear plausible on the surface and so, the question that will be asked here is, do these theories inform us about the historical development of social inequalities and challenge exploitation or do they simply justify oppression? Historical examples of religious, biological, cultural, social, economic and feminist theories which justify oppression will be examined. Then, a contemporary theory on inequality which actually informs us about the historical development of social inequality and challenges exploitation will be discussed. This is the black socialist feminist theory. This chapter illustrates that in order to understand inequalities in society, we need to examine the history of how some people have become rich and others have been made poor. This requires a study of social, economic and political relationships through history between the haves and have-nots, between the powerful and the oppressed. Making sense of inequalities in society and inequalities in society's institutions, such as education, is then possible.

If the examination of certain historic forces enables us to have some insight into the unequal position that some groups of people hold in society, what role do schools have in offering students opportunities to learn about these forces? This is a question that will be explored in the following chapters, but first, let us examine some of the theories that have been developed in the past to explain social inequalities.

Many religions, for example Hinduism, Islam and Christianity, have been used by certain groups of people in society for the purposes of explaining social inequalities related to class, race, gender and sexuality. The following examples are taken from the dominant religion in Britain.

During the feudal period in Britain, the nobility did not socialise with the 'common people' (Worsley, 1984). They married within their own circles, thus maintaining a safe distance between themselves and the toiling masses. The nobility explained their privileged position through religion, asserting that the peasants were supposed to be descendants of Ham, who for lack of filial piety, was known to have been condemned to slavery by Noah. The peasants were thus seen to be worthy only of a slave-like existence, presumably with God's blessing. This theory was expressed in religious worship, for example, the hymn, 'All things bright and beautiful' does not only rejoice in all creatures great and small and all things wise and wonderful for the 'Lord God made them all', it also explains that:

> The rich man in his castle,
> The poor man at his gate,
> God made them high or lowly,
> And ordered their estate.
> (Hymn No. 573, in Monk, 1875, p. 814)

Certain interpretations of the *Bible* reinforced by such hymns served to disguise the exploitive relationship that the lords and ladies had with the labouring class. Such religious explanations gave very little concrete information about the oppressive element of the relationship. It did not explain how the nobility became rich and why the majority of the hard-working people lived on the brink of starvation.

When Britain embarked upon its colonial mission, the ideology of God ordering high and low estates was transported abroad and the story of Ham was reproduced. This time, African people were seen as descendants of Ham, condemned to slavery and to remain 'hewers of wood and drawers of water'. Notions of Africans being ungodly and depraved contributed towards the belief that the transportation of millions of Africans to the plantations of the New World was almost an act of Christian charity. Such religious justification for the enslavement and colonization of millions of human beings once again disguised the exploitive relationship that existed between Britain and its ever expanding empire (Fryer, 1984).

Regarding the position of women in society, there is a story in the book of Genesis that says that the original sin in the Garden of Eden was a woman's. She tasted the forbidden fruit, tempted Adam and the Lord said:

> I will greatly multiply thy sorrow and thy conception; in sorrow thou shalt bring forth children; and thy desire shall be to thy husband, and he shall rule over thee. (Genesis, Chapter 3, verse 16, *Bible*, Revised Standard Version, 1952)

This biblical story continues to have a powerful influence on many people today as it offers them an insight into the unequal positions held by women and men in society. According to this perspective, since God has decreed that women shall be the slaves of men then there has to be some spiritual meaning and divine purpose for this difficult but unavoidable situation.

Similarly, religion has been used to explain and justify the oppression of lesbians and gay men. For this purpose, the Letter of Saint Paul to the Romans is often referred to. In Romans Chapter 1 verses 18 to 27, Saint Paul explains that 'For the wrath of God is revealed from heaven against all ungodliness and wickedness of men who by their wickedness suppress the truth . . .' Among this group of the wicked, Saint Paul placed lesbians and gay men and called them the people of 'dishonourable passions'. Saint Paul explained that 'Their women exchanged natural relations for unnatural, and the men likewise gave up natural relations with women and were consumed with passion for one another, men committing shameless acts with men . . .' For such acts, Saint Paul explained that the wicked would receive their own due penalty (Romans, Chapter 1, verses 18 to 27).

This biblical story like the story of Adam and Eve continues to have a powerful influence as it offers some groups of people a legitimate right to oppress lesbians and gay men. This perspective views homosexual relationship as wicked and denies the possibility for love and respect in lesbian and gay relationships (Bishop Shelby Spong, 1989).

Besides looking to God to make sense of social inequalities, some theoreticians have homed in on the 'culture of the poor' and produced the culture of poverty theory. The idea of certain cultures themselves producing poverty is well illustrated in the work of an American anthropologist Oscar Lewis. After studying the poor in Mexico and in Puerto Rico, Lewis argues that the culture of poverty is a 'design for living' which is transmitted from one generation to the next. Lewis goes on to assert that the people in the lower strata of society have certain characteristics which render them to feelings of marginality, helplessness, dependence, inferiority, thoughts of living only in the present with relatively little ability to defer gratification, a sense of resignation and fatalism, and so forth. Lewis also explains that by the time children from the slums are 6 or 7 years old, they have usually absorbed the basic values and attitudes of their culture and are not psychologically geared to take full advantage of changing conditions or increased opportunities which society may have to offer (Haralambos, 1980, pp. 154–5).

According to the culture of poverty theory, therefore, poor people are seen to perpetuate their own poverty through their culture. Cultural norms, values and behaviour are seen as being internalized and passed on from one generation to the next, thereby producing the next group of people who do not quite make it. Poor people are seen to be gripped by such a powerful way of life that they cannot snap out of it in order to take advantage of the range of opportunities that are supposedly available equally to all people in society and simply reproduce the next generation of poor.

Michael Harrington, who has a similar perspective to that of Lewis, writes in *The Other America* that among the American poor, there is a language of the poor, a psychology of the poor, a world view of the poor. Harrington argues that to be impoverished is to be an internal alien, to grow up in a culture that is radically different from the one that dominates the society (Haralambos, 1980, p. 155).

Such is the perspective that looks at a group of people's 'internal deficiencies', in this instance, their culture, in order to explain and justify social inequalities. By focusing on poor people's culture to explain their position, wider socio-economic processes are effectively ignored.

Social theoreticians who have focused on the culture of people that are poor have influenced education too. The theory of cultural deprivation suggests that the whole culture of low-income groups is deprived and deficient in important respects, and this accounts for the low educational attainment of members of these groups. The so-called culturally deprived child is seen to be deficient and lacking in important skills, attitudes and values needed for educational attainment.

The cultural deprivation theory has influenced education policies, particularly in the sixties and seventies. Having located the problem of the low educational attainment of working-class students within their culture, these education policies argue that equality of opportunity can only become a reality by compensating for the cultural deprivation and deficiencies of working-class people.

The theory of cultural deprivation lays behind many education programmes instituted both in Britain and in the USA. In Britain, compensatory education began in the late 1960s with the government allocating extra resources for schools in the inner cities. In the United States, the compensatory education programme took the form of 'Operation Head Start' under President Lyndon Johnson. The major aim of both the Compensatory Education and the Operation Head Start programmes was to instil achievement motivation (which was seen to be lacking in working-class children), through planned enrichment and a stimulating educational environment (Bilton *et al.*, 1981, pp. 438–40).

In the 1970s, the cultural deprivation theory influenced many social scientists who were examining the position of black people in Britain. This time it was the turn of black people to have their culture examined by interested analysts. The classic in this field, is *Endless Pressure* (Pryce, 1979). In his book, Pryce adopts a participative observation method for collecting data on the life-styles of a Jamaican community living in a provincial British city. Pryce argues that there are seven groupings among this Jamaican community. These are the 'hustlers', 'teenyboppers', 'proletarians', 'respectables', 'saints', 'mainliners' and 'inbetweeners'. The seven groups are categorized as adopting one of two major 'life orientations': the 'stable law abiding orientation' and the 'expressive disreputable orientation'. The essential difference between the two lifestyles is employment. Pryce argues that the people in the stable law abiding orientation earn their money legally through employment while the people with a disreputable life style 'hustle', prostitution being the main form of hustling.

Among the young Jamaicans, Pryce identifies a group of teenyboppers and describes them as: 'West Indian youth ... male ... homeless ... unemployed and at risk, either a delinquent or in danger of becoming one' (Pryce, 1979, p. 109). He argues that the cause of the teenybopper problem is related to the teenyboppers' family structure, their cultural deprivation and their lack of a grounded sense of identity. Pryce also states that 'the West Indian child is severely handicapped and cannot make the tremendous adjustment necessary to remedy the deficiencies in his socio-cultural background, which he must do if he is to take full advantage of the educational opportunities open to him in his new metropolitan environment' (Pryce, 1979, p. 120).

By basing his work on the theory of cultural deprivation, Pryce effectively manages to pathologize the culture of an oppressed group. By avoiding an examination of the historical, political and economic experiences of black people, Pryce offers a distorted picture of the present social and cultural life styles of Afro-Caribbean people living in Great Britain. The reproduction of such racist stereotypes fuels racism, lends support to the oppression of black people and does little for 'improving race relations'.

While some analysts have focused on the culture of oppressed people in order to explain the position that they hold in society, others have looked at wider social processes to explain inequalities in society. These are the structural functionalists and they generally assume that social phenomena exist because they have some positive function to perform in society. According to functionalists, even poverty has a positive function in society. Davis and Moore (1945) express this point clearly. They argue that some positions in society are functionally more important than others and require special skills. People differ in terms of their 'innate ability and talent'. Those that do have the talent have to make sacrifices and 'differ gratification' in order to go for training prior to taking up vital positions in society. The talented will only be induced to train if they are ultimately given sufficient rewards. The rewards and their distribution become a part of the social order and thus give rise to social inequality (Davis and Moore, 1945, pp. 242–9).

According to the functionalist perspective, social inequality has been a prominent feature of past human societies and continues to be so because it performs a necessary and positive social function. The functionalist perspective does not explain how and why in Britain in the 1980s for example, 10 per cent of the population owned four-fifths of all personal wealth (Bilton, *et al.*, 1981, p. 68) nor does it shed much light on the ever widening wealth gap between the rich and the poor in Britain of the 1990s (Townsend, 1993, Whitehead and Dahlgren, 1991). The assertion that the greatest rewards are offered to the most skilled and talented people is not sufficient to explain such a distribution of wealth. If we accept the functionalist perspective, we would have to accept that the wealth is distributed in this manner because 'innate' talent is sparse among 90 per cent of people in Britain. The people at the top of the hierarchy are overwhelmingly white upper- and middle-class men. If we accept the functionalist perspective, we would have to agree that there is no class, race and gender oppression in this society.

Besides arguing that poverty has a positive function in society (where some people have innate talent and others do not), structural functionalists also assert that gender divisions in society have a biological base. According to Parsons, for example, the fundamental explanation of the allocation of roles between the biological sexes lies in the fact that 'the bearing and early nursing of children establish a strong presumptive primacy of the relation of mother to the small child' (Haralambos, 1980, p. 372). Because of the bond that women have with their babies, Parsons argues that the obvious role for women in society is a nurturing one. Parsons sees the role of women in society as providing warmth and emotional support to their children in order to ensure effective 'socialization'. Men, according to Parsons, work hard in a competitive world and this causes them stress and anxiety. The other role of women is therefore to provide consideration, understanding and love to their husbands, so that the stressed and exhausted breadwinners can calm down and 'stabilize'. Thus the two functions of the nuclear family in modern industrial society: the socialization of the young and the stabilization of adults, are fulfilled.

Biology therefore is the starting point for Parsons in his explanation of sexual division of labour. This perspective does not acknowledge that women are oppressed, in fact the unequal positions held by women and men are seen as natural. The argument that there are natural biological roles for women and men in society is restrictive of both women and men. It does not make any allowances for women to develop their full potential as creative intelligent human beings outside their reproductive and nurturing role. Moreover, this perspective does not offer men the possibility to express themselves as loving and caring human beings. The role allocation according to this perspective encourages and justifies women's economic dependency on men and other forms of sexual oppression.

Biological explanations of social inequalities have been constructed to justify various forms of inequalities. During the last century, for example, the position of poor people in Britain was often explained in terms of their 'hereditary characteristics'. The classic in this field is a study by Charles Booth. In 1887, Booth studied the inhabitants of Tower Hamlets and wrote about the conditions in which the people lived, the nature of their employment or unemployment, and their life-styles. Booth divided the population of this large part of London of the 1880s into many sections and divisions, and described the social context of each group in great detail. This study has become renowned for illustrating the extent of poverty that existed in London in the nineteenth century. Many remember Booth for what they think was his humanitarian concern for the poor and the destitute. He wrote, 'I am deeply in earnest in my desire that the conditions under which the mass of the people live should be improved' (Booth, 1887, p. 375).

On examining Booth's research closely, one finds Booth's views of the most destitute and impoverished group with no regular wages. Booth argues that the people in this group,

> consist of casual labourers of low character . . . they degrade whatever they touch, and as individuals are almost incapable of improvement; they may be to some extent a necessary evil in every large city, but their numbers will be affected by the economic conditions of the classes above them and the discretion of the 'charitable world'. (Booth, 1887, p. 334)

Booth's understanding of the cause of poverty amongst this group of people is illuminative. He asserts that 'it must be desired and to be hoped that this class may become less hereditary in its character. There appears to be no doubt that it is hereditary to a very large extent' (Booth, 1887, p. 335).

We see that while Booth expressed concern about the destitute in nineteenth century London, he argues that the poor are poor because of some hereditary characteristic, and that there was little hope for them. This is one example of a biological explanation for social inequalities. Like the religious theory, such biological explanations offer little hope for the oppressed position of workers with no regular wages. By focusing on people's biological makeup, attention is effectively taken away from the socio-economic forces which make it possible for a small group of people to own the wealth of a nation while the majority work for a pittance.

Biological theories have also been used to justify the colonization and the exploitation of black people. 'Scientists' in nineteenth century Britain were arguing that African people were 'naturally' inferior to the Europeans:

> I am apt to suspect the negroes . . . to be naturally inferior to whites. There never was a civilised nation of any other complexion than white, nor even any individual, eminent either in action or speculation. No ingenious manufacture among them, no arts, no sciences. On the other hand, the most rude and barbarous of the white, such as the ancient Germans, the present Tartars, still have some thing eminent about them in their valour, form of government or some other particular. Such a uniform and constant difference could not happen, in so many countries and ages, if nature had not made an original distinction betwixt these breeds of men. (Fryer, 1984, p. 152)

Black people were portrayed not simply as naturally inferior to Europeans but as being closer to animals:

We cannot pronounce them unsusceptable of civilisation since even apes have been taught to eat, drink, repose and dress like men. But of all the human species hitherto discovered, their natural baseness of mind seems to afford least hope of their being (except by miraculous interposition of Divine Providence) so refined as to think as well as act like men. I do not think that an orang-outang husband would be any dishonour to an Hottentot female. (Carter, 1966, pp. 15–16)

Such opinions dressed up as scientific theories were used for the justification of the systematic implementation of slavery, genocide and colonialism for the purposes of building Britain. These theories disregarded the fact that the peoples of Africa have a long and a rich history of creativity and sophisticated expressions of life through language, music and art. These theories disregarded the fact that in Africa there existed a great civilization that has made a major contribution to the ancient civilizations of India, Greece and Rome. These theories disregarded the fact that prior to the European invasion of Africa, the peoples of Africa lived in various group forms ranging from the small self-sufficient village communities to the large city states with complex political, social and economic systems.

When the question of education for black people in the United States became an issue at the beginning of this century, some educationalists focused on the genetic make-up of black people. Ferguson, for example, in *The Psychology of the Negro: An Experimental Study* (1916), asserts that the genetic make-up of black people contributes towards them being intellectually inferior to white people. Black people were considered capable only of physical labour, and so Ferguson and others suggested that the education provision for black people should aim to develop black people's sensory motor powers and so avoid 'great waste' of the country's resources.

Biological explanations for the 'intelligence quotient' of black people did not exist only in United States at the turn of this century. In Britain Eysenck, a senior member of The London Institute of Psychiatry, made a major contribution to this 'science' in the 1970s. Eysenck expressed concern that 'among the problems which face humankind, that of race is one of the most difficult, . . . if we do not solve it sooner rather than later, it threatens to engulf us in strife . . . which will make previous wars and commotions seem trivial'. (Eysenck, 1971, p. 8). It is this concern that led him to research into the education needs of black people and conclude that there is much evidence to show that black people are on the average 'inferior to whites' on many diverse tests and that a considerable portion of this difference is genetic in origin (Eysenck, 1971). By focusing on the genetic make-up of black students in order to explain their position in white schools, attention is diverted from the operation of racist policies and structures within the education systems.

I have touched briefly on theories that mask reality and justify various forms of oppression. Radical feminism in Europe and the United States developed as a direct challenge to such theories about women. Interestingly, radical feminism is also based on a biological explanation (see, for example, Firestone, 1972). This particular feminist theory argues that men are biologically aggressive and violent, and women, as child bearers, are biologically nurturing, caring and loving. According to this perspective, the exploitation of women by men that has arisen out of biological differences — patriarchy — is the source of all oppressions, for example capitalism, colonialism, etc. While other feminist perspectives define patriarchy as one of many forms of oppression ultimately based on socio-economic forces, radical feminism views biological patriarchy as the oppression which gave birth to all other oppressions. Radical feminism argues that if patriarchy is overthrown, then the other oppressions will not have a basis for existence. To put it in other words, if the skeleton of the monster is smashed then the whole beast will surely die.

This analysis seems coherent and convincing; after all, sexism is endemic at all levels of society and among all nationalities of people. Also, women throughout history have been oppressed and exploited by men. Nevertheless, if we look beneath the surface of the radical feminist perspective, we see glaring gaps and inconsistencies. The radical feminist perspective on racism is illuminative.

Since men are seen as being naturally aggressive and violent, according to radical feminism, colonialism is simply viewed as a male activity and adventure. Colonialism is seen as another system of oppression set up by men, this time European men. European women are seen as being used by the men to maintain this oppressive system. If this argument was valid and European women really were forced to uphold colonialism, why is there so little evidence of European women challenging or organizing against colonialism? (Hooks, 1982, p. 125). History illustrates that wherever force has been used to oppress a group of people, one of the reactions of the oppressed group is to resist their oppressors.

Even though the political economic relationship between Europe and its colonial territories is denied in many ways by radical feminists and other theoreticians, the reality of colonialism remains. Colonialism was not simply a brief (male) hiccup in history. European colonialism began five hundred years ago and continues today through insidious new forms — neo-colonialism of the 'independent' ex-colonies. Colonialism has resulted in the exploitation of a substantial proportion of this world's peoples — women, men and children, and their land. From this exploitation, European men and women of all classes have profited and continue to profit. Of course, not all Europeans have gained equally. The European upper-class men gained the most. European upper-class women gained more than the working-class men, and the European working-class women gained the least. The colonial gains are not incidental, trivial or even gains only of the past. Colonialism is related directly to some countries being rich and developed, while many countries are poor and under-developed. It is no accident that people in some countries live on average long, comfortable lives while the majority of the people in other countries live difficult, short lives:

Life expectancy in years:

The longest lived			*and the shortest*		
	1987	**1992**		**1987**	**1992**
Japan	78	78.6	Afganistan	42	42.5
Canada	77	77	Ethiopia	42	45.5
Netherlands	77	77.2	Sierra Leone	42	42
Norway	77	77.1	Guinea	43	43.5
Spain	77	77	Angola	45	45.5
Sweden	77	77.4	Mali	45	45
Switzerland	77	77.4	Niger	45	45.5
Australia	76	76.5	Central African Republic	46	49.5
UK	76	75.7	Chad	46	46.5
USA	76	75.9	Somalia	46	46.1

(1987 figures from *New Internationalist*, No. 200, Oct. 1989;
1992 figures from *United Nations Human Development Report* 1992)

The interfaces between race, class and gender oppressions is complex, and theoreticians have taken various positions about this throughout history. Orthodox Marxists argue that class oppression is fundamental and race and gender oppressions are elements of class contradictions. This position does not recognize the complexity of the oppressions experienced by black people and women. Radical feminists state that sexism is the primary oppression which has given birth to all other forms of oppression. This position has contributed little to the liberation of working-class and black people — black women and working-class women included. Some black nationalists on the other hand argue that the liberation of black people and their land is the priority. When this perspective overlooks class and gender contradictions, in the long term, it can obstruct the liberation of women and working-class people.

Black socialist feminists have produced a comprehensive analysis on the complex dynamic of oppression and domination (see Bhavnani and Coulson, 1986; Hooks, 1982, 1989, 1992; Parmar, 1982). They assert that the oppression of all women cannot be eradicated while some systems of oppression stay intact; in the struggle for a better world, all systems of domination have to be confronted. Increasingly, black socialist feminists have rejected the notion that the overthrow of patriarchy or capitalism alone will end all oppressions. Black socialist feminists do not deny that contradictions exist between black and white women, between working-class and middle-class women, between

15

black women living in Europe and black women living in the underdeveloped, colonized countries, between lesbians and heterosexual women. They recognize that women are not equally oppressed. They acknowledge that while all women are oppressed, some groups of women have greater privileges and power compared to some groups of men. In short, black socialist feminists do not hold a linear analysis of oppression.

This chapter has so far examined several theories on social inequality. If we restrict our focus to one particular inequality in society, the unequal position of black students in the education system, which perspective offers the greatest potential for understanding this phenomenon? First, it is not constructive to explain the position of black students in religious terms and assert that white people as citizens of 'Babylon', a corrupt land, are depraved people and therefore evil and oppressive. A biological explanation which asserts that black students are oppressed because of the biological make-up of white people is not adequate either. A depoliticized cultural explanation is also not appropriate. Such an explanation could assert that white people with a great culture are best equipped to rule most of this world and that black people are not oppressed, they simply do not have the appropriate culture to make progress and take up prestigious positions in this world. Finally, the functionalist perspective which argues that social and educational hierarchies are necessary for the well-being of the society because they ensure that people will work hard for greater rewards, is also inaccurate — middle-class white men are not the only hard-working group of people.

Biological, religious, narrow cultural explanations and functionalist perspectives are thus not adequate for explaining inequalities within the education system or within society. Black socialist feminism, on the other hand, does offer a greater potential for a thorough examination of the position of black students in the British education system and other disadvantaged groups in society. This perspective focuses neither on the biology or the culture of people in order to explain inequalities nor turns to gods for explanations. It accepts the multi-faceted nature of oppression, that is, the dynamics of the forces of race, class, gender and sexuality. In short, the black socialist feminist perspective turns to the roots of oppression and examines the political economy of inequality in relation to all oppressed groups through history in order to make sense of inequality in society today. Thus black socialist feminists turn to a specific history in order to make sense of the present.

With regards to the oppression and inequality experienced by black students in British schools, the black socialist feminist perspective would examine the relationship between the British state and black women, men and children through history. Certain questions would be central to such an examination. When, why and how did the contact between Britain and black people first begin? How has the socio-economic and political relationship between Britain and black people developed through history? How has this relationship contributed towards the present position of black people in Britain? Only when such historical issues are explored can we begin to understand the position of young black people in British schools today. Without such an understanding and acceptance of black students, it is not possible to respect black students or to have a constructive relationship with them in the education context. Chapter 2 will therefore explore issues related to black history and ask what aspects of this history ought to be acknowledged and taught in schools.

Chapter 2

The Unmasking of Black History

You may write me down in history
With your bitter twisted lies
You may trod me in the very dirt,
But still like dirt I'll rise . . .
. . . Into a daybreak that's wonderously clear
I rise
Bring the gifts that my ancestors gave
I rise, I rise, I rise . . .
(Maya Angelou, 1984)

Chapter 1 illustrated that history offers an important key to understanding the inequalities experienced by groups of people in society today. In order to understand the present position of black students within the British education system, it is necessary to examine the relationship that the British state has had with black people through history. Certain questions are central to such an examination. When, why and how did the contact between Britain and black people first begin? How did this contact develop? This chapter will outline some of the significant elements of the historical relationship between Britain and black people, taking into account the specific relationship between Britain and black women. In doing so, it will be clear that a substantial part of Britain's contact with black women, men and children has been based on slavery, indentured labour and colonialism, and that black people have made a major contribution towards the development of Britain. The history of the relationship between Britain and black people is rarely acknowledged and is generally hidden. Since the knowledge of black history is necessary for understanding black students, the unmasking of black history raises the question of how much of this history ought to be taught in schools.

The Transition of European Feudalism to Capitalism

Contact between Europe and the countries of black people increased dramatically as the European economy began its shift from feudalism to capitalism. The development of capitalism in Europe was based on the accumulation of capital by means of exploiting human labour. This process of exploitation was first carried out within Europe itself. Land that had been previously held in common during the feudal era was enclosed as private property. A large group of landless peasants was thus cut away from the traditional mode of production. This dispossessed group of people, without the means of subsistence, was forced to live by selling its labour. Furthermore, within Europe itself, throughout the eleventh, twelfth and thirteenth centuries, Europe's population grew and wastelands and swamps were cleared to cultivate more food. The frontiers of Christian Europe itself were pushed out. The German and Scandinavian peoples for example conquered and converted the Baltic and Slavic peoples. Cyprus, Crete, Palestine and Syria were conquered in the Crusades. In Britain, there was English expansion into Wales, Scotland and Ireland. In this way, strategies adopted for relocation, deportation and expropriation were practised within Europe before overseas colonial expansion was carried out (Worsley, 1984, Institute of Race Relations, 1982).

Britain was the first country to complete the massive shift from a feudal economy to a capitalist one. This could not have been possible without the wealth that was created through the British Empire. What should young people in schools be taught about Britain's industrial revolution? Should they be told that the industrial revolution in Britain was the result of the new and sophisticated methods of farming and other inventions which made mass production possible? Should they be taught the names of the people who invented machines in Britain and the dates of these inventions? Or should history students be encouraged to examine the process by which Britain acquired the wealth which lay the foundations for the revolution? The great inventions and the liberating ideology of the Reformation were indeed important factors in the transformation of the British feudal society. However, it was the capital that was accumulated from the slave trade, the plantation economy and the Indian colony that made the most significant contribution towards Britain's industrialization. As Winston Churchill said in 1939:

> Our possession of the West Indies, like that of India ... gave us the strength, the support, but especially the capital, the wealth, at a time when no other European nation possessed such a reserve, which enabled us to come through the great struggle of the Napoleonic Wars, the keen competition of the eighteenth and nineteenth centuries, and enabled us ... to lay the foundation of that commercial and financial leadership which ... enabled us to make our great position in the world. (Fryer, 1988, p. 4)

In the fifteenth century, Spain, Portugal, Britain, France and Holland were involved in the conquering and the colonization of huge sections of America. The colonization of many of the countries of central, south and north America by the western European nations contributed towards the development of Western Europe and the underdevelopment of the American colonies. The plantation system was one avenue which made this process of wealth transfer possible. The plantation system was set up, not for the benefit of the local people, but for the purposes of creating wealth for the European settlers who controlled the crops produced. By the seventeenth century, the plantation system became a massive operation requiring a labour force which could not be met by the local diminished populations or by the group of paupers, prisoners and indentured labourers transported from Europe. Thus the European plantocracy began to look to Africa for this extra labour. From the middle of the seventeenth century, the trade in African slaves to work the tobacco and then the cotton plantations of North America, the mines, coffee, cocoa and sugar plantations of Latin America, and the sugar plantations of the West Indies grew until it reached massive proportions both in terms of profit and of people (Dunbar Ortis, 1984). And so, a new chapter in the history of Europe unfolded and Africa lost millions of her people.

Britain's Trade in Human Beings

Several European countries were involved in the buying and selling of African people for slave labour and if we focus on Britain's role in this trade, we find that by the eighteenth century, Britain became a dominant force in this commerce. Sir John Hawkins transported the first 'cargo' of 300 slaves from West Africa to the Caribbean island of Hispaniola (now Haiti) in 1562 for Britain. By 1713, under the Treaty of Utrecht, Britain acquired from France the contract to supply African slaves to the Spanish colonies. After this, Britain became a leading slave carrier for other European countries and the centre of the Triangular Trade (Bryan, Dadzie and Scafe, 1985). Slavery is often viewed as an unpleasant activity of a handful of eccentric British men. Rarely is the slave trade examined as a massive operation which contributed significantly to the development of Britain and other European countries that profited from the slave trade and the underdevelopment of the countries of Africa which lost a substantial section of their most productive labour force. For these reasons, the history of British slavery needs to be situated within the political economic context of development and underdevelopment.

The inhumanity of slavery can be traced through the various traumas that the slaves had to endure before they began work on the plantations, if they survived the crossing from Africa. African people were rounded up and chained together. Next, there was the long march to the west coast, which many did not survive. Once there they were sold for guns, spirits and cotton goods and stowed away on board ship like cargo, packed in the minimum of space in order to maximize the number of slaves transported per journey. The long voyage across the Atlantic Ocean, the 'middle passage', also resulted in many deaths (Bryan, *et al.*, 1985, p. 6). Over the 300 years of the slave trade thousands of Africans died during this journey. For the slave owners, however, such deaths were not a great loss, as they were able to make a claim for compensation from the insurance companies (Rodney, 1970).

On board the ships, the men captives were crammed in fetid darkness in the hold twenty hours a day. They were allowed on deck once a day to be hosed down, fed and then to be made to dance to preserve their physique. In stormy weather, or if there was any hint of a rebellion, they were kept in the hold all the time. The women captives on board the ships were greatly exploited. They were in a minority, as they constituted about 20 per cent of the people who were transported as slaves. During the voyage across the ocean, they were kept separately from the African men in order that the sailors could exploit them sexually. Apart from some rare exceptions, there is evidence that most women slaves were sexually abused during their traumatic sea voyage away from their homes. The experience of personal violence for the women slaves did not end on arrival in the New World. African women were bought, not only for the purposes of labouring as field workers and domestic servants, but also for the sexual gratification of the plantation owners, the managers and the overseers. Above and beyond this, the women slaves experienced sexual abuse from the male slaves, as well (Tinker, 1974, p. 11). Finally, particularly after the legal ending of the slave trade in 1807, the women slaves were expected to produce the next generation of slaves when the popular plantation maxim, 'it is cheaper to buy than to breed', could no longer be upheld. It was the resistance of the women slaves that ensured that the new generations of slaves were not produced as fast as the planters had hoped (Bryan, *et al.*, 1985).

Many countries in Europe benefited from the slave trade, and Britain, who had a monopoly of this trade, gained the most. The average price for the slaves was £80 in the late eighteenth century, and in Cuba in the nineteenth century, planters paid between £200 and £250 for a slave (Tinker, 1974, p. 5). The sugar and the cotton that the African slaves produced on the plantations in the Americas provided employment in Britain's developing refining and manufacturing industries. The surplus products from Britain were then shipped back to Africa to purchase more slaves, thereby beginning the whole triangular trade cycle again. The overall benefits from this venture were enormous and eventually turned Britain into the strongest trading nation in the world. The slave trade and the plantation economy made a major contribution towards Britain's lead in the industrial revolution.

The slave trade was a massive operation; it was not a hobby or a passtime of a handful of eccentric European entrepreneurs. Many African lives were lost. W. Rodney explains that any figure of Africans imported to the Americas which is based only on the surviving records is bound to be low because there were so many people who had a vested interest in withholding such data. Indeed there are no records of the slaves who were smuggled or who never landed in the Americas alive. Rodney suggests that between 1445 and 1870, Africa lost between 40 and 50 million people, as a result of the slave trade and associated activities, while 15 million Africans landed alive (Rodney, 1970, p. 104). Once the slaves landed alive in the Americas, despite the 'seasoning' period, between one-quarter and one-third of the new arrivals died in the first years (Tinker, 1974, p. 5). The consequences of the slave trade for Africa's demography were therefore immense. While the population of Europe during the period of the slave trade increased, the population of Africa was drastically reduced. The slave trade deprived Africa of its most productive labour force.

The economic, social and political consequences of the slave trade were also far-reaching for Africa. This trade created conditions in Africa which were hostile to the process of economic transformation and development. For Britain, on the other hand, the capital accumulated from this trade in human beings formed the basis of its industrial revolution and related development (Bryan, *et al.*, 1985).

Justifications for the Buying and Selling of Human Beings

Europeans justified this trade in human beings in numerous ways. The more profitable this trade became, the more rationalizations supporting such a practise had to be formulated. The belief that asserted that it was all right to uproot a people from their country by force, transport them across the sea to an alien part of the world, sell them as slaves and make them work from sunrise to sunset for no wages began to be reflected in many parts of the European society. Indeed religion, literature and other institutions of sixteenth century Europe soon absorbed these ideas.

Religious justifications that were put forward in order to make the buying and selling of human beings an acceptable activity are a significant, though another ignored element of British history. Conveniently, the story of Ham was used once again. This time, it was the turn of the Africans to be the descendants of Ham, 'the black son' of Noah. As such, Africans were seen as natural slaves, condemned forever to remain 'hewers of wood and drawers of water'. With such an ideology, it was possible to catalogue human beings along with livestock and to treat them as work animals. People sang hymns about how all things were bright and beautiful . . . the lord God made them all . . . the rich man (the master) in his castle, the poor man at his gate (the slaves in their hovels) . . . God made them high or lowly, and ordered their estate (Biko, 1978, p. 29). Religion was thus a powerful purging mechanism for the guilt that may have been experienced by the beneficiaries of this trade for their 'man's inhumanity against man', (women and children included).

Such justifications for the exploitation of black people have contributed towards a powerful European ideology, namely, racism. This racism is not the same as prejudice. Indeed all groups of people have prejudices and myths about other groups of people. However, the ancient prejudices and myths that the British and other Europeans had about black people were brought together to form a coherent ideology from the sixteenth century onwards. This ideology was not simply passed on by word of mouth as prejudices tend to be, it was backed initially by religion, then later by 'science' and became institutionalized in various European social structures, such as literature, the law and social policy. European racism, therefore, is not the same as any other prejudice. European racism does not simply assert that European people are superior and that non-European people are backward, it has justified the domination of a very large proportion of the world's population through imperial rule and continues to justify the oppression of black people today.

British racism is a significant part of Britain's relationship with black people. If we focus on the British brand of European racism we find that in the literature of sixteenth century Britain, the words black and white were heavily charged with meaning. Blackness in England has traditionally stood for death, mourning, evil, sin, baseness and danger. Other meanings of the word 'black' included: deeply stained with dirt, soiled, foul, having dark or deadly purpose, malignant, pertaining to death, disastrous, sinister, horrible, wicked. People spoke of black arts, blackmail, Black Death, the devil himself was black, and so, the logic ran, all black people were devils. Embedded in this concept of blackness was its direct opposite, whiteness, supposedly the colour of purity, innocence, and perfect human beauty (Fryer, 1984, p. 135).

Thomas Heywood, a playwright, referred to 'a Moor, of all that beares man's shape likest a devil' (Fryer, 1984, p. 136). Devils, monsters and beasts were the images of African people during the flowering of English literature in the early decades of the slave trade. In the words of the new merchant capitalist, we see the dehumanizing of the African, the reduction of a human to a commodity for sale — a slave. The exploitation of human beings through a system of slavery gave rise to the institutionalization of racism in Britain and other European countries that benefited from slavery.

It is usually suggested that the abolition of slavery was achieved as a result of a humanitarian movement spearheaded by such individuals as William Wilberforce. Teaching in schools tends to perpetuate this version of events (Bryan, *et al.*, 1985). However, there were many factors which led to the breakdown of the system, and the agitation of black and white humanitarians was only one of them. Owning and maintaining rebellious slaves was becoming more expensive than hiring and firing 'free' workers. Central to the abolition of slavery was the resistance which the slaves put up (Reynolds, 1985). The successful slave revolution in St Dominique (now Haiti), led by Toussaint L'Ouverture, sent a shock-wave through Europe and did much to undermine the morale of planters on the other islands in the Caribbean.

The racist ideology which was used to justify slavery was indeed quite versatile, and it was not long before it was adapted for the purposes of colonizing. In 1792, Charles Grant, a British historian, was calling the Indian people, 'a race of men lamentably degenerate and base, retaining but a feeble sense of moral obligation ... governed by a malevolent and licentious passion ...' And this 'race of men' was commonly referred to by the British as 'blacks'. Another term originating from African slavery, 'nigger', was also applied to Indians. By the 1850s, Indians were described as 'the wild barbarians, indifferent to human life . . . yet free, simple as children, brave, faithful to their masters', by the historian Herbert Edwards. This could well have been a general description of African slaves by their white master (Hiro, 1971, p. xvi).

In 1899 Rudyard Kipling exhorted his fellow country people to

Take up the white man's burden
Send forth the best ye breed
Go bind your sons to exile
To serve your captive's need;
To wait in heavy harness,
On fluttered fold and wild
Your new caught, sullen peoples,
Half devil and half child. (Kipling, 1977, p. 128)

Britain's Trade with India

While wealth was pouring into Britain from the slave trade and the slave plantations, Britain was extending its trading links with many countries in Africa and in Asia. India was seen by the British as the 'jewel in the crown' of her ever-expanding empire. The history of the relationship between Britain and India is also significant in terms of the development of 'Great' Britain. Some details of this history are worth noting.

The Portuguese were in fact the first Europeans to establish trade with India in 1498. The French and the Dutch followed. In 1600, a British trading company called the East India Company was formed and its aim was not to 'serve the captives' needs', but to take over the immensely profitable trade from its European rivals. Initially, Britain had surplus wealth for the purposes of trading fairly with the Indian merchants for Britain had a regular supply of silver bullion from Spain. Britain acquired the silver that Spain plundered from the Americas by supplying almost 5000 slaves a year to Spain. This supply of silver gave Britain an advantage that the other European traders in India did not have (Dutt, 1940).

This fair trade with India did not last long. In 1608, the East India Company, with the use of its own private army, dispersed a Portuguese squadron off Surat and persuaded the local ruler to allow the Company to build a permanent depot there. This strategic base allowed the British to control the Arabian Sea and the Persian Gulf. Similarly, the East India Company, with the help of the royal British troops, dispersed the French and took control of the East coast of India in 1751. Bengal's ruler's resistance against British domination resulted in the Battle of Plassey in 1757. Once Britain won this battle and secured a strong base in India, it embarked on another mission. Britain converted its trade with India into plunder (Muk-herjee, 1974).

In May of 1762, the Nawab of Bengal complained to the English Governor that members of the East India Company were forcibly taking away the goods and commodities of the Indian peasants and merchants for one-fourth of their value. Similarly, an honest English merchant, William Bolt, in his 1772 paper, 'Considerations on Indian Affairs' wrote that the East India Company, besides fixing very low prices for Indian commodities, arbitrarily decided what quantities of goods Indian merchants should produce. Weavers who were employed by the company were given low wages, and if the weavers protested, they were flogged. If these weavers wanted to subsidize their wages, they were not allowed to work for anyone else. Bolt stated that the 'roguery practised in this department is beyond imagination; but all terminates in the defrauding of the poor weaver' (Dutt, 1940).

Britain's Gift to India — Landlessness, Poverty and Famines

By treachery and conquest, much of India came under the Company's direct rule. Once India was carved up by the East India Company, the avenues for extracting wealth out of India and into Britain multiplied. The Company introduced private ownership of land in Bengal, Bihar and Orissa. Before Britain's intervention in India, the land belonged to the cultivators of that land. For centuries Indian people had a particular relationship with their land, they worked on it and saw it as a sacred source of life. A portion of the cultivators' crop was collected by a Zamindari (collector of revenue) on behalf of and for the Indian authorities. Most importantly, the cultivators paid according to the amount of crop that they had produced. When the harvest was poor, the Zamindaris collected a smaller portion of the cultivators crops — the Indian rulers had compassion for their people. A substantial part of the surplus collected from the cultivators was used for public facilities for the villagers, for example, schools, health centres, irrigation systems, roads, etc. Village artisans and manufacturers were also paid for their labour by agricultural produce (Hensman, 1971).

The land system introduced by the British in India was designed to increase the revenue for Britain. This was done by making the Zamindaris, the previous land revenue collectors, into owners of land who had to pay taxes to the British authorities. Thus two groups of people were created in India: a small group who owned the land and the masses who lost all rights to that land. In this way, the fundamental relationship that the Indian people had with their land was changed. The land on which people had assumed that they could live and work was made transferable at the will of the new owner and could be inherited, mortgaged and generally treated as a commodity. Many people were forced to become landless and rural indebtedness increased rapidly (Hensman, 1971). Such was the 'civilizing mission' of Britain in India.

Although India had an abundance of fertile land, many of its people became landless and poor. Indeed, under the new rulers, the cultivators had to pay taxes even in times of drought. This the Indian workers of the land had to do by borrowing money from money lenders (Mukherjee, 1974). As Britain continued to develop into a mighty and a glorious nation, India was being transformed into a destitute land of despair. Under the British administration of India, the number of famines soared from seven in the first half of the nineteenth century to twenty-four in the second half. Millions of Indian women, men and children lost their lives. In Bengal alone in 1770, one-third of the peasantry died of starvation (Fryer, 1988, pp. 19–20).

Britain's 'Free Trade' with India

It was in the nineteenth century that Britain systematically destroyed India's textile industry. This was done on the basis of one-way free trade. One-way free trade meant that there was virtual free entry for British goods into India while tariffs were imposed against the entry of Indian goods into Britain and the prevention of direct trade between India and other countries. Such navigation acts were passed and imposed by Britain in most of her colonies. In this way, the predominance of British textile goods was built up and the Indian manufacturing industry destroyed (Porter, 1984). For Britain, therefore, India was important as a supplier of raw cotton as well as a market for her goods.

Between 1814 and 1835 British cotton goods exported to India rose from less than one million yards to over 51 million yards. In the same period, Indian cotton goods imported into Britain fell from one and a quarter million pieces to 306,000 pieces and by 1844, to 60,000 pieces. By 1850 India, which for centuries had exported cotton goods to many countries, was importing one-fourth of all British goods (Dutt, 1940). This process was carried on through the nineteenth century and even into the twentieth century (Mukherjee, 1974). Alongside the development of Britain was the under-development of India.

What should history students learn about the historical relationship between Britain and India? Should they learn about the dialectical nature of development and underdevelopment through imperialism? Should they learn about the sophisticated textile industry that existed in India prior to the 'British Raj'? Should they learn about the manner in which the British destroyed the Indian textile industry for the purpose of building its own textile industry? Or should the students simply learn about the trade between Britain and India during the period of the British Empire as requested by the National History Curriculum?

Britain's Control of India

The plunder of India was not achieved easily: the Indian people mounted formidable resistance against their colonizers. Britain was, however, able to curb this resistance effectively because of its advanced military technology. Thus, India was forcibly transformed from being a country with a rich agricultural economy and a strong industrial base into a dependant colony of Britain.

While history lessons in schools sometimes give the impression that Britain ruled many countries because the people of these countries were somehow incapable of governing themselves, little information is given in history lessons as to how Britain managed to gain control over its empire. Ruthless and violent strategies were adopted and resistance was often curbed viciously. How many British pupils know of the massacre of people who had peacefully gathered at Jallianwallah Bagh, Amritsar in 1919? (Ali, 1983, p. 15). Three hundred and seventy-nine people were killed and 1200 people wounded. Besides such unleashing of violence, the British adopted other tactics to retain control.

> The Indigo Commission's report showed that the plantation system in Bengal was slavery under another name. Ryots (peasants) who objected to sowing indigo were murdered; their houses were pulled down; they were kidnapped and locked up; their cattle were seized; their very gardens were grubbed up to make room for indigo. (Fryer, 1988, p. 23)

Against such brutality Indian resistance grew and culminated in a great upsurge in 1857. This uprising, India's first national war of independence, shook the British Empire to its very foundation. This war spread through a vast area of India (the size of France, Austria and Prussia together) with a population of 45 million (at a time when Britain was inhabited by 28 million people). For over a year the Indian people put up a remarkable resistance and Britain almost lost its jewel. Britain retaliated ruthlessly and won this war by butchering thousands of Indians. Sir John Kaye in *History of the Sepoy War in India* described this succinctly. He wrote:

> our military officers were hunting down criminals of all kinds, and hanging them up with as little compunction as though they had been pariah dogs or jackals, or vermin of a baser kind. . . . Volunteer hanging parties went onto the districts, and amateur executioners were not wanting to the occasion. One gentleman boasted of the number he had finished off quite 'in an artistic manner', with mango trees as gibbets and elephants for drops, the victims of this wild justice being strung up as though for pastime, in 'the form of a figure eight'. (Kaye, 1864–76, pp. 170, 235–7)

There was much bloodshed, and many Indian and even British people died. The Indian national uprising failed primarily because the British had better war weapons — the newly invented Enfield rifle and access to a good communication system — the telegraph. Furthermore, the British sacrificed one year's worth of Indian revenue — 36 million pounds, to suppress the Indian War of Independence (Fryer, 1988, pp. 23 and 111). To consolidate this expensive gain, the British government suspended its indirect rule of the sub-continent through the East India Company and forced direct control upon India. Amidst the plunder of India, Indian people kept their resistence alive until Britain finally withdrew on 14th of August, 1947.

It was rarely acknowledged in Britain that the forceful hold over the countries of other people was for the economic development of Britain. Most British intellectuals believed with pride that their countrymen were civilizing primitive and savage peoples of this world who did not know how to govern themselves. On Sundays, many British people rejoiced and sang and prayed to God for strength to fulfil their great mission in this world:

From Greenland's icy mountains,
From India's coral strand,
Where Afric's sunny fountains
Roll down their golden sand,
From many an ancient river,
From many a palmy plain,
They call us to deliver
Their land from error's chain.

What though the spicy breezes
Blow soft o'er Ceylon's isle,
Though every prospect pleases
And only man is vile,
In vain with lavish kindness
The gifts of God are strown,
The heathen in his blindness
Bows down to wood and stone.

Can we, whose souls are lighted
With wisdom from on high,
Can we to men benighted
The lamp of life deny?
Salvation! oh, salvation!
The joyful sound proclaim,
Till each remotest nation
Has learn'd Messiah's name.

Waft, waft, ye wind, His story,
And you, ye waters, roll,

Till, like a sea of glory,
It spreads from pole to pole;
Till o'er our ransom'd nature
The lamb of sinners slain,
Redeemer, King, Creator,
In bliss returns to reign.
AMEN
(Monk, 1875, p. 500).

By 1830 the Industrial Revolution which had changed the material prosperity of Britain had left India economically poor. She was no longer a large scale supplier of cotton goods to Europe, she was a consumer of British products. The slump in the cotton industry and massive landlessness resulted in wide-scale unemployment. India was ripe for exploitation by the planters in the slave-owning colonies, for once slavery was abolished, the planters sought new sources of cheap and plentiful labour.

Britain Creates a New System of Slavery

From 1830 to 1920, the recruitment of Indian people to work on the various plantations of the British and French colonies was organized through what became known as the indenture labour system. This system resembled slavery in many aspects and has been referred to as 'the new system of slavery'. This neglected area of the history of Britain's relationship with Indian people has been well researched and documented by Hugh Tinker (1974).

To the landless and the unemployed Indian, emigration offered hope of employment and a better life. British companies employed Indian men to tour villages where the crop had failed or where unemployment was high, in order to recruit indentured labourers. The recruiter or 'Kangani' promised bright futures in the land of plenty that awaited them overseas. The journey from the villages to the Indian ports was long; for example, the journey from Patna or Benares to Calcutta took thirty to forty days, and had the manner of a forced march. Many arrived at the depot in very poor condition. At the depots the recruits had medical examinations. Sight and hearing were tested, but above all, the ability to use heavy agricultural equipment was checked. Once the medical checks had been made, contracts were signed. Men were recruited for five years, and women were recruited for three. Since the depots could handle only a limited number of ships at a time the recruits had to live in difficult and cramped conditions for up to six weeks before they set sail to the land of their dreams. Yet despite such conditions, few changed their minds because the Kanganis constantly told them stories of the wonderful life that lay ahead of them.

The passage to the colonies was a harrowing experience for the Indian emigrants. As on the slave ships, these 'coolies' were packed in a small space in order to maximize the number of labourers transported. Sanitary conditions were poor, the water supply was filthy and food was sparse. Many died en route. An 1857 ship of 385 indentured labourers to British Guiana resulted in 375 people falling sick, out of whom 120 Indians actually died (Tinker, 1974).

Many new emigrants arrived in the colonies in debt, mainly a result of their not having enough money to pay for the sea voyage. The Kangani kept a record of the debt and collected it from the labourers' meagre wages. Furthermore, the wages were paid in arrears and were subjected to stoppages because of absence or uncompleted work. The pay was poor and the Kangani gave just enough to the labourer to stay alive. Thus the labourer was never out of debt. Planters in Ceylon during the 1850s paid labourers four to six pence a day, while in Java they were paid one-and-a-half pence a day (Tinker, 1974).

Death and sickness on the plantations took their toll of both men and women, who usually arrived physically unwell or weak, after the difficult sea voyage. Since the planters had the labourers indentured for a limited period, the newly arrived labourers were not given time to recover and get acclimatized, they were expected to start work immediately. If the labourers did not do sufficient work, money would be deducted from their wages. The former slaves' accommodation was generally used for the labourers. It was basic, was not much different from the barns used for the cattle, and the term 'Nigger Yard' continued to be used to refer to the labourers' dwellings. Indeed, as there was little opportunity for family life, most labourers spent what little rest time they had in drunken oblivion.

The women indentured labourers, like their African sisters who were enslaved, were in the minority. The women experienced sexual violence both en route to the 'land of their hopes' on board the ships, as well as in the 'countries of their dreams' (Tinker, 1974, p. 204). The women indentured labourers were not seen simply as field and domestic workers, they were also expected to be sexually available to their employers and fellow labourers. In fact, because there were fewer women than men, a certain form of polyandry was developed. This meant that one man would accept a number of male 'lodgers' in his room, and one woman, his domestic servant, was required to cook for them and be sexually available to all of them.

The other role of the women labourers was to reproduce new labourers. Most women were loath to bring children into their world. Birth rates remained low in all the colonies with an indenture labour system, not only because of the widespread practice of abortions among the women, but also because of the poor conditions which led to a high neonatal mortality rate. If a woman did give birth, she had a brief period of rest before she and her newborn were expected to be out in the fields:

> A coolie woman gets a variable amount of leave for her confinement.
> After that, if the infant is not strangled at birth, she must either take
> it out with her to her work or leave it behind, with no one to look

after it. In the former case, tied to its mother's back, or left in the nearest drain, it is exposed to extremes of heat and cold . . . in the latter, the child gets half starved . . . or succeeds in cutting short its career by a fall. . . . (Tinker, 1974, p. 206)

And yet, many children were born and survived. They grew as best they could. Few went to school, for there were almost no schools on the estates. At the age of ten they had to join the weeding gangs, and as soon as the law permitted they were indentured. Such was the life of the children of the indentured labourers.

This new system of slavery was carefully designed to extract maximum labour for a minimum outlay. Laws were set up to ensure this. The indentured labourers had no escape. They were totally bound to their master, the plantation owner, for they were held criminally liable for even the slightest breach of their contract. Absence from work (even due to sickness) for seven consecutive days was regarded as desertion and was punishable, in British Guiana for example, by a fine of $24 or one month's imprisonment with hard labour. In Trinidad, the maximum penalty for this crime was two months imprisonment. For the use of threatening language against an overseer, negligence or the hindering of other labourers in their work, an indentured labourer could be fined £5 or jailed for two months. In this way it was hoped that resistance would be 'nipped in the bud'.

There were, however, numerous cases of small groups of labourers rebelling. Often these protests would be sparked off when the plantation owners tried to impose restrictions, for example, refusal of a holiday or a reduction in wages. The protests were always put down with severity, and even when the labourers were granted some of their demands, their leaders were always singled out for punishment. Because of the successful organization of repression, the rise of mass protests was slow in the colonies operating an indenture system (Tinker, 1974).

After the legal ending of slavery in 1833, the labour of the indentured Indians saved the sugar economy in Trinidad and British Guiana. This profitable coolie system was extended to most of the British and French colonies, for example East and South Africa, Guyana, Sri Lanka, Malaya, Fiji and Mauritius. In spite of the significant contribution of the Indian indentured labourers to Britain's development, this element of history has been effectively eradicated. Should British students be offered an opportunity to explore this part of Britain's past?

The British Administered Genocides

That Britain has been involved in wholesale destruction of many groups of people of her colonies is rarely acknowledged. During the period of the British Raj in India, Tasmania, Australia, New Zealand and South Africa, were also being conquered by the British imperialists for the purposes of extending the Empire. Britain played a leading role in the appropriation of the land of the Tasmanians, Australians, New Zealanders and the Southern Africans. In order to do this, military and gun warfare tactics were employed. The people from these lands mounted formidable resistance against the invaders, for their land was their ancestral heritage for their community. This resistance was curbed by the British, who slaughtered vast communities and placed the remainder on reservations (Porter, 1984).

Tasmania, Australia and New Zealand were conquered and settled by the British for the primary purposes of finding opportunities for its burgeoning unemployed and convict community. The takeover of these countries was ruthless. Women, men and children were pitilessly hunted down, tortured and put to death. Tasmanians were tied to trees and used as targets for shooting practice. The flood of the British immigrants into Tasmania caused such a severe food shortage that hundreds of Tasmanians died of starvation. The genocide of the people of Tasmania was completed within seventy-five years of the first British settlements in 1803 (Fryer, 1988, p. 38).

When Captain Cook arrived in Australia, he found generous, warm people. Yet after the arrival of the British in Australia, the population of Australia decreased from 300,000 in 1788 to 77,501 in 1921 (Fryer, 1988, p. 39). At least 20,000 Australians were killed in warfare. Australians were also killed by poisoning with arsenic or strychnine mixed in flour, while many died from the invasion's secondary effects: disease, disruption and starvation (Fryer, 1988).

The Australians resisted the invasion of their land fiercely. Despite having only spears against the British guns, this warfare lasted almost 160 years from the first battle at Sydney in 1770 to the last massacres in the Northern Territory in 1930 (Institute of Race Relations, Book Two, 1982, p. 4). This undeclared war against the Australian people ended after the colonial authorities agreed to allow some of the remaining militant tribes access to small patches of (state controlled) land.

British sovereignty over New Zealand was proclaimed in 1840 when systematic colonization began. The social organization of the New Zealanders enabled them to mount extensive resistance to the colonialists and the British troops had to be called in to overcome this resistance.

The population of New Zealand was estimated at between 125,000 and 175,000 before the British invasion. Within a hundred years, it had been reduced to an estimated 45,000. Here too, systematic warfare, disease and starvation were the major causes of this mass destruction (Fryer, 1988, pp. 41–43).

Justifications for the Mass Destruction

How was it possible for British people to carry out such massacres of the people of Tasmania, Australia and New Zealand? Such atrocities had to be justified somehow, but how? Did Britain not stop the slave trade in 1807?

Did Britain not outlaw slavery in 1832? Did this not mean that Britain was a country concerned about humanity? How then was it possible for British people to kill so many human beings and rob their land? The answer is that the survival of the empire that was built on slave labour depended on the continuation of ruthless exploitation of others for its own sake.

The abolition of slavery did not mean that the racist ideology which supported slavery was dismantled. Racism was far too valuable to be dispensed with. We have seen through the case of India how the British racism was transported to the colonies of the ever-expanding British Empire. When it came to the expropriation of the land of the peoples of Tasmania, Australia and New Zealand, the old racist ideology had to be further refined. After all, according to Genesis, God had said that the black son of Noah and his descendants shall be enslaved, he had not said that black people should be the targets of genocide.

Murdering vast populations of human beings was justified in Britain in scientific terms. Scientists aimed to prove that there exists a natural, biological hierarchy among human beings. These scientists took Darwin's revolutionary theory about the evolution of nature as their starting point. They argued that evolution is a process in which the fittest species survived and developed, and others were left behind. Although Darwin himself did not apply his findings to human societies, many scientists did, and they asserted that Europeans are the fittest, strongest, most intelligent and thus most powerful of human races. All other people were ranked in order behind the Europeans. The conclusion of this 'scientific' theory was that inferior races do not survive in the struggle of mankind, for a higher intellectual and deeper emotional life; it was unfortunate but understandable that some of the 'primitive' races disappeared as the more advanced races developed. Such racist ideology was used to justify the massacres of the peoples of Tasmania, Australia, New Zealand and South Africa. This British science grew and developed rapidly in the eighteenth century.

Eighteenth century anthropology, the study of human societies, offered sketches of Africans, Europeans and others. Europeans were described as being of 'fair complexion, sanguine temperament, and brawny form . . . of quick manners, accurate in judgement, of quick invention, and governed by fixed laws . . .' Black people on the other hand were described as 'crafty, indolent and of careless disposition, . . . governed in their actions by caprice . . .' (Fryer, 1984, p. 166).

Phrenology aimed to study human intelligence through the examination of human skulls. The leading phrenologists had a large collection of human skulls from all over the world. These scientist firmly believed that there was a correlation between the shape of the head of different human groups and their degree of civilization. In 1819 the distinguished surgeon, Sir William Lawrence, used his collection of skulls to argue that race and culture were connected. Lawrence asserted that 'the Negro structure approximates unequivocally to that of the monkey' (Lawrence, 1819, pp. 476–493).

In nineteenth century Britain, racism was widespread among the scientists and intellectuals, the majority of whom took it for granted that only people with white skins were capable of thinking and governing. Hunt's Anthropological Society, for example, was founded in 1843. Within two years it had 500 members, mostly medical men, lawyers, journalists, clergymen and colonial administrators. Among other things, Hunt's doctrine asserted

> that the analogies are far more numerous between the Negro and the ape, than between the European and the ape, that the Negro is inferior intellectually to the European, that the Negro becomes humanized when in his natural subordination to the Europeans, that the Negro race can only be humanized and civilised by the Europeans and that the European civilization is not suited to the Negro's requirements or character. (Hunt, 1863–64, pp. 51–52)

Such 'science' justified empire building. This racist pseudo-science was based on racist myths and totally disregarded the fact that one of the oldest civilizations of this world existed in Africa and that the people of Africa have a long history of creativity (Bernal, 1987). The British and other European pseudo-scientists told their fellow people that they were ruling over races which, unlike themselves, were lacking in intelligence. The scientist of this persuasion argued that the extinction of the inhabitants of many parts of the Americas was nature's way of making room for a higher race. This evolutionary racism in Britain in the nineteenth century encouraged the 'native policy' for Tasmania, Australia, New Zealand, South Africa and Canada (Fryer, 1984, p. 166).

Towards the end of the nineteenth century, as Fryer illustrates in detail, the British people took it for granted that Europeans were the top race. The Colonial Secretary, Joseph Chamberlain, said in 1895,

> I believe that the British race is the greatest of governing races the world has ever seen. (Cheers)
> I say this not merely as an empty boast, but as proved and shown by the success which we have had in administering vast dominions . . . I believe there are no limits accordingly to its future. (Fryer, 1984, p. 182)

Britain's Creation of Apartheid in South Africa

Having become 'the greatest of governing races the world has ever known', the relationship between Britain and the countries of black people deepened. Indeed there were no limits for Britain, and parts of Africa were to become her next possession. It was in fact the Dutch who were the first Europeans to go to South Africa in 1652 with a view to settling there. It did not take long before vast communities of Africans were made landless, reduced to a state of poverty and used as slave labour (Porter, 1984).

British colonialism became the dominant force in South Africa after the Anglo-French wars of 1793–1815. Apartheid was constructed under the leadership of Sir Theophilus Shepstone, who served as the British diplomatic agent in Natal 1845–1875 and put into operation extensive segregation policies. In 1913, the Native Land Act gave apartheid the force of law, thus legally taking away all the rights of the African people, restricting them to only 13 per cent of the poorest land and offering them extremely harsh conditions of employment (Davidson, 1983). What role do British history teachers have in teaching their students about the oppression of apartheid and Britain's historic contribution towards the establishment of apartheid?

Britain's 'Trade' with Africa

It is not only with South Africa that Britain has a significant historical relationship. Britain, along with several other European nations, has had, and continues to have, an unequal relationship with the rest of the rich and vast continent of Africa. This has contributed towards the development of Europe and the underdevelopment of Africa (Rodney, 1972).

Long before the colonial era, the slave trade was a basic factor in the underdevelopment of Africa. Other facets of unequal trading between Africa and European countries (Britain included) led to further underdevelopment of Africa. As in India, European traders destroyed the African cloth handloom industry. Two policies were adopted to achieve this end. First, the distribution of African cloth was carefully controlled by European trading companies and second, the African market was flooded by bulk manufactured cloth from Europe. Africa, like India, was exporting raw cotton and importing manufactured cotton cloth by the nineteenth century (Davidson, 1983).

Britain Shares Africa

Such unequal trade between Europe and Africa encompassed numerous commodities and lasted four centuries before a single more systematic colonial system was established. At the Berlin Conference of 1885 Africa was divided into 'spheres of influence' among the leading European imperialist nations, Britain, Germany, Belgium, France, Italy, Portugal and Spain. The aim of this carving up of Africa was to ensure that the conflict between the colonizing powers was minimized, thereby enabling each of these European countries to invade a part of Africa within its sphere of influence.

Each of the European powers in Africa adopted its own method of conquering and colonizing Africa. Britain, drawing upon its rich experience of empire building, adopted two major strategies for colonizing countries in

Africa. Essentially, two types of colonies were created — settler colonies and non-settler colonies. In the settler colonies, the most fertile land was taken from the Africans by the British settlers. Once the land was taken, most British people were not prepared to work on this land themselves, and African labour was used. Various methods were adopted to exploit this labour. In all the British colonies, the violent form of forced labour was used to make Africans to work for the British. If they refused, they were tortured (Rodney, 1972). This resulted in much suffering and many African deaths. Because the Africans resisted strongly, more subtle and effective strategies were adopted through the implementation of a tax system.

Britain's Gift to Africa: A Comprehensive Tax System

Africans were made to pay taxes to the British authorities for their land, their huts, even their fish and their cattle. Taxes had to be paid in the form of money which could only be obtained by labouring for the British on the British-owned farms, in the British-owned mines, building mansions for the British settlers and working on the roads, railways and ports which were to be used for expropriating African resources out of Africa (Macdonald, 1981).

Africans employed by the British generally did not have decent contracts of employment. Africans were often employed on temporary basis for eight to ten months thereby having few if any rights, for sick and annual leave, etc. The majority of men were forced to work long distances away from their families and communities. This caused great strain on the workers and their families and communities. Going to work did not mean prosperity for the Africans; indeed many lives were lost through illnesses and accidents related to employment. Between 1900 and 1933 more than 30,000 African workers lost their lives in Northern Rhodesian mines, approximately 3000 by accidents and 27,000 by diseases caught at work (Davidson, 1983, p. 15). This process of creating wage-workers was described by an African trade-unionist, J.H. Mphemba (1929):

> First the White man brought the Bible, then the white man brought guns, then chains, then he built a jail, then he made the natives pay tax. (Davidson, 1983, p. 14)

The waged labour system had many of the characteristics of the indentured labour system and was almost as harsh as slavery. The workers were forced into employment. Kwame Nkrumah outlines how the workers were paid wages in theory, but three-quarters of their wages were deferred until the end of their contract, and then the taxes were deducted. The taxes were so high that at the end of the period of employment many workers had no balance at all (Nkrumah, 1963, p. 39).

Walter Rodney in *How Europe Underdeveloped Africa* outlined clearly the wage differentials for workers in the African colonies and Europe. Wages paid to workers in Europe were higher than wages paid to African workers even for doing exactly the same work. Rodney illustrates how the records of the large American shipping company, Farrel Lines, show that in 1955, of the total amount spent on loading and discharging cargo moving between Africa and America, five-sixths went to American workers and one-sixth to Africans. It was, in fact, the same amount of cargo that was loaded and unloaded at both ends! Another example cited concerns coal mining in Nigeria and Scotland. The Nigerian coal miners at Enugu earned one shilling per day while the Scottish coal miners doing the same job earned the same amount in an hour. The point that needs stressing is that the wages paid to the European workers were such that the capitalists still made a profit. The rate of exploitation of the African workers, like the workers in other colonies, was far greater than the exploitation of European workers (Rodney, 1972, pp. 163–4).

Why such inequality? Was it, as many colonial administrators believed, that African people living in the 'jungles' did not have as sophisticated lifestyles and needs as the Europeans and therefore required less income? Economic and cultural imperialism has contributed towards some countries being developed today and others being underdeveloped. Should history students in Britain be offered the opportunity to explore such issues or should their teachers ignore this history, thereby reinforcing the racist stereotype that some countries are backward because their people are ignorant?

Britain's Gift to Africa: The Cash Crop System

Britain, like the other colonizing nations, used numerous strategies to extract the wealth out of the colonies; the establishment of the cash crop system is an example. In the case of Africa, farmers were forced into producing such crops as cocoa, ground nuts, palm kernels, cotton and coffee for the export market. Crops grown on African land with African labour were sold by European traders who fixed the prices and reaped the profits. By paying the labourers low wages, crops were produced cheaply. This produce was then sold at high prices in Europe:

> . . . the West African Produce Board paid Nigerians £16.15s for a ton of palm oil in 1946 and sold that through the Ministry of Food for £95, which was nearer to the world market prices. Ground nuts which received £15 per ton bought by the Board were later sold in Britain at £110 per ton. (Rodney, 1972, p. 185)

For the British people and other European colonizers, there were huge profits; for the African farmers, indebtedness grew steadily because their production costs were not covered by their wages. In many colonies, which were forced into a cash crop system, increasing pressure was exerted on local farmers to produce for the cash crop industry. In this way, less food was produced for the local people. Thus began the process which later contributed towards famines in many British and other European colonies (Rodney, 1972 and Sivanandan, 1989).

Britain's Gift to African Women

Colonialism contributed towards a deterioration in the status of women in many areas of their life. One example is in agriculture. Prior to European rule women in many colonies had control of the agricultural sector, since they were primarily responsible for cultivation and distribution. Men were responsible for other areas of work, for example, felling trees, hunting and defence. Esther Boserup illustrates in her book, *Women's Role in Economic Development*, how European settlers, colonial administrators and technical advisers have been largely responsible for the deterioration in the status of women in the agricultural sectors of developing countries (Boserup, 1970, pp. 53–4).

The British, like their European counterparts, showed little sympathy for the female farming systems which they found in many of the colonies. While women in pre-colonial societies did experience sexism, they nevertheless had a certain amount of power within their own societies. British colonialists operating with a different sexist framework reproduced Anglo-centric hierarchies in the countries where they ruled and actively undermined colonized women's spheres of influence.

In many parts of Africa, prior to the the European invasion, women had control of the production and distribution of food crops. The British administrators assumed that farming was a man's job and that men make superior farmers. Thus they showed little respect for the female farming systems that they encountered in the colonies and promoted male farming to replace female farming. Men were given greater responsibility for farming. When new agricultural methods were introduced, only men were instructed, women were ignored. As the gap in knowledge and training widened between men and women, men's prestige improved at the expense of women's. The position of male farmers was further enhanced by giving men decision-making powers while the role of women was reduced to that of hired workers or family aids. Finally, women lost their right to own land, as the land was taken over either directly by the British administrators or transferred to men (Boserup, 1970).

British colonialists objected to the position and role that African (and Asian) women held outside their families, for they were unlike current Victorian values. The Victorian notion that women's role in life was only to take care of their families in their homes was thus transported to the 'dark continents' during the civilizing missions. In this way, the gender divisions of labour were changed in colonial societies, often to the detriment of women (Hooks, 1981).

Women did not relinquish a significant area of their world and life without resisting. There are many recorded cases of women rebelling against their oppressors. One such revolt was launched in the Kon region of Eastern Nigeria in 1959. The women organized this protest in response to the deterioration of their position as farmers, coupled with their fear of losing their land to male farmers. During the uprising, some 2000 women, led by the traditional women's organization in the region, marched in procession to a neighbouring town, occupied the market and set fire to it. They agreed on a number of resolutions — among these, the elimination of all foreign institutions, such as courts and schools, and the expulsion from the region of all foreigners. The unrest among the Kon women spread to neighbouring tribes (Boserup, 1970, pp. 63–64).

'Progressive' history books and books about the history of people, as opposed to books about kings and queens, generally overlook the particular experience of women through history. Even studies that look at colonialism and its impact on working class and black people often do not examine the specific impact of colonialism on women. While colonialism was and is a ruthless oppression against all colonized peoples, the particular oppression of women is significant. By assuming that the experience of colonialism for women and men was the same, a significant part of history is masked and gradually eradicated. Do schools have a role in ensuring that black and white women's history is not eradicated?

Having briefly examined the historical relationship between Britain and black people during the age of the great British Empire, it is clear that over the last five hundred years, black women, men and children have made a major contribution towards the development of Britain. It was slavery and colonialism that helped to make Britain 'Great'. By 1900, British colonies and dependencies exceeded thirteen million square miles, of which the United Kingdom accounted for less than one-hundredth (Gundara, 1982, p. 44). The experience of colonialism for black people was not an enlightening one, it was essentially oppressive. British colonialism resulted in the development of Britain and the underdevelopment of all the countries in its empire.

Black People in Britain Today

Having looked at the historical relationship between Britain and black people, we arrive at the question of black people in Britain today. Why are there black people living in Britain? Has the relationship that was once based on exploitation changed? The popular thinking is that black people have come to the richer, advanced countries of Europe in order to improve their economic position, since life in their poor 'backward' countries is difficult. Although it is true that black people have travelled all over the world in search of employment and a better life, we need to ask why it is that their countries are poor while other countries are rich. Popular explanations of the black presence in Britain do not consider this question and so reinforce the racist notion that black people are 'scroungers', who have foisted themselves onto this land with green pastures.

If we examine the dialectical relationship between rich and poor countries, we find that integral to this relationship is a history of migration. The growth of European capitalism has been dependent upon the movement, sometimes forcible, of large numbers of workers (Tierney, 1982, p. 19). This systematically organized movement of people has been from the rural areas into towns within Europe during the early stages of capitalism, from Europe into the colonies during the colonial period, and more recently, from the ex-colonies and poorer parts of the Mediterranean into the richer countries of Europe.

From the 1940s onwards, Britain has had to surrender most of its colonies. This was mainly due to Britain's inability to contain the widespread resistance and armed struggles that were sweeping through its empire (Porter, 1984). The two World Wars had left Britain with a shortage of labour and unemployed and landless black people from Britain's ex-colonies were invited to work in the 'Mother Country'. The black people living in Britain today are the descendants of the African slaves, the Indian coolies, the landless farmers and the unemployed labourers of the British Empire (Porter, 1984).

When black people arrived in Britain after the war, the areas of work that were mainly open to them were in the factories, mills, foundries and on the buses (Sivanandan, 1982). In the recession of the 1990s, a disproportionate number of black people are either in low-paid employment or have no employment at all. It is not only in the area of employment that black people experience discrimination; racism has no boundaries and often black people suffer inequalities even in the 'caring' institutions of our society, for example, within social, welfare and health services. Occasionally the media reports about black people who are murdered on the streets, in their own homes or in their school playground and this raises the question of how many black women, men and children are harassed and intimidated on a daily basis because of their race?

An examination of Britain's relationship with black people through history thus clearly indicates that the relationship is an unequal one and that the basis of Britain's relationship with black people has been, and still is, exploitation. This exploitation is justified and upheld by an ideology of racism (Fryer, p. 1984).

Enslaving and colonizing a people involved ruthless determination and violence on the part of the slavers and colonizers. The enslaved and colonized were treated as less than human, a race closer to animals. The rich history and culture of black people was totally denied and systematically invalidated by the new, civilized and civilizing rulers. Then began the process of indoctrination; a process which attempted to instil in black people the idea that they are inferior, that the European way of life is the best and that Europeans are best equipped to govern the countries of this world. This cultural imperialism was a subtle method used by the enslavers and colonizers for gaining and retaining power. If this strategy did not work, then force, various tortures and punishments were used. For women, there was always the threat of sexual violence. These methods of terrorizing succeeded in forcing many slaves and colonized people to repress their awareness of themselves as free, intelligent and creative people (Hooks, 1981, p. 19).

Rodney argues that

> the colonial education system was not an education system designed to give young people confidence and pride as members of African societies, but one which sought to instil a sense of deference towards all that was European and capitalist. (Rodney, 1972, p. 17)

Indeed this applied to the education systems established by the British in all their colonies.

The denial of the history and the identity of black people was an important strategy used by the British and other Europeans to enslave and colonize black people. Today, many British people believe that Britain is a free, egalitarian and a democratic country which respects human rights. If this is the case, to what extent does the British education system offer respect to black people by acknowledging black people's contribution towards the development of Britain and by affirming black people's rich history of creativity and struggles for justice? The next chapter examines the extent to which the major education policies of this country acknowledge black history.

Chapter 3

The Denial of Black History in the National Education Policies

Undergraduates, seduced, as always, by the changing breath of journalistic fashion, demand that they should be taught the history of black Africa. Perhaps, in the future, there will be some African history to teach. But at present there is none, or very little: there is only the history of the Europeans in Africa. The rest is largely darkness, like the history of pre-European, pre-Columbian America. And darkness is not a subject for history.

... If all history is equal, as some now believe, there is no reason why we should not study one section of it rather than another, for certainly we cannot study it all. Then indeed we may neglect our own history and amuse ourselves with the unrewarding gyrations of barbarous tribes in picturesque but irrelevant corners of the globe ...

It is European techniques, European examples, European ideas, which have shaken the non-European world out of its past — out of barbarism in Africa, out of a far older, slower, more majestic civilisation in Asia; and the history of the world, for the last five centuries, in so far as it has significance, has been European history. (Hugh Trevor-Roper, now Lord Delcare, 1966, in Chirimuuta and Chirimuuta, 1987)

It is such disregard for the independent history of black people and the history of the political economic relationship between Britain and black people that has legitimized racism and continues to contribute towards the oppression of black people today. Historically, the denial of the history and the identity of black people was an important strategy used by the British and other Europeans to enslave and colonize black people.

Black people have a long history of creativity and struggles for justice, and unless this history is acknowledged, it is not possible to offer black students understanding, acceptance and respect. This chapter examines the extent to which the major education policies of this country, in their efforts to help black students, acknowledge black history and the great contribution of black people to Britain and the rest of the world through the ages. The next chapter will examine the National History Curriculum (England) to ascertain what possibilities there are within this British state-imposed legislation to explore and celebrate the history of black people with black and white students in schools. But first, let us look at the antecedent to the National History Curriculum.

Over the last three decades, various governments have requested special committees to examine the needs of black students and to suggest strategies for improving the position of minority groups in the education system. How did the committee members analyze black students? Did the members of the committees consider it necessary to examine the history of black students in order to understand the position of young black people in schools today? What recommendations did they make for improving the position of black students within the education system? To what extent do the members of the committees concerned about black students offer respect to black people by acknowledging black people's contribution towards the development of Britain and by affirming black people's rich history of creativity and struggles for justice?

During the fifties and the sixties black people were generally perceived as being different and in need of help to assimilate into the British society. The thinking behind the idea of assimilation was that if black people were to give up their 'peculiar' customs and adopt the British way of life, they would be treated as equals.

It was the Commonwealth Immigrants Advisory Council (CIAC), appointed by the Home Secretary, that laid the foundation for the assimilation strategy in education. The members of this committee experienced problems as they planned assimilation for black people. The CIAC explained that, even though half a million immigrants represent a small proportion of the total population of Britain, 'these immigrants are visibly distinguishable by the colour of their skins...' (CIAC, 1964). Besides the anxiety about the colour of Asian and African people living in Britain, the Council expressed concern about the 'habits' and customs of black people, and the education of 'children of unfamiliar background' was seen to present 'real difficulties at a time when classes are already overcrowded'.

Having explained that black peoples' lifestyles hinder the progress of students, this Advisory Council recommended that the national system of education must aim at 'producing citizens who can take their place in society properly equipped to exercise rights — perform duties which are the same as those of other citizens'. The Council had no hesitation in recommending that if the parents of children in schools live their daily lives with a culture that is not 'British', then, the children should be encouraged to respect their parent's culture 'but a national system cannot be expected to perpetuate the different values of immigrant groups' (CIAC, 1964).

The aim of education, according to the Council's perspective, was therefore to assimilate black students into a fair and egalitarian society supposedly having no class, gender or race inequalities. Clearly the Council's anxiety was that if values other than the mainstream British values were fostered, then conflict would be created both within the education system and society at large. For these reasons, an attempt was made to systematically eradicate black identity, history and language, thereby reinforcing eurocentric, sexist, middle-class values.

A year later in 1965, the Department of Education and Science (DES) echoed the CIAC's approach defining the task of education as 'the successful assimilation of immigrant children' (DES, 1965). At the same time, the Labour government was concerned about the number of black people in Britain and passed the Commonwealth Immigration Act (1964). This act aimed to control the number of black people entering this country, since Britain had accumulated a sufficient reserve army of cheap labour. With the reassurance from the Labour government that it would do all it could to curtail the flow of black people into Britain, the DES proceeded to formulate strategies for the assimilation of black students into the education system.

The procedure for assimilating black students was outlined by the DES in circular (7/1965), *The Education of Immigrants.* In this circular, under a section headed, 'Spreading the children', teachers were notified that, 'It is inevitable that, as the proportion of immigrant children in a school or class increases, the problems will become more difficult to solve, and the chances of assimilation more remote' (DES, 7/1965, p. 4). The concentration of black students in schools was clearly perceived as undermining the process of assimilation.

In this 1965 document, the DES argued that 'up to a fifth of immigrant children in any group can fit in with reasonable ease, . . . if the proportion goes over one-third either in the school as a whole or in any one class, serious strains arise'. The fear of black students swamping the education system gave rise to the DES recommending that 'the catchment areas of schools should, wherever possible, be arranged to avoid undue concentrations of immigrant children'. Where this proved impracticable simply because the school served an area which was occupied largely by black people, the DES asserted that 'every effort should be made to disperse the immigrant children round a greater number of schools and to meet such problems of transport as may arise' (DES, 7/1965, p. 4).

Thus hundreds of black children were bussed daily to schools long distances away from their homes. Dispersal of black students reduced contact between black parents and their children's schools, but this did not concern the DES. The priority for the DES was the interest of white parents who were reassured that every measure would be taken to ensure that their childrens' education would not be hindered by the presence of too many foreigners in schools. The only italicized passage in the DES circular stated that 'It will be helpful if the parents of non-immigrant children can see that practical measures have been taken to deal with the problems in the schools and that progress of their own children is not being restricted by the undue preoccupation of the teaching staff with the linguistic and other difficulties of immigrant children' (DES, 7/1965, p. 6).

Neither the Commonwealth Immigration Advisory Council nor the Department of Education and Science acknowledged the identity or the history of black students. Black students, with their supposedly strange habits and customs, were seen, not only as a problem, but also as a threat, threatening to disrupt the education of the white students. Furthermore, it was assumed that the presence of black students would inevitably lead to a lowering of education standards. Instead of schools being encouraged to respect the identity, culture and history of every student, the educational aim became an endeavour to spread black students thinly on the ground and to make them pure 'British'.

The acquisition of the English language was considered to be an important route to successful assimilation. English was not only to be taught to black children in schools, special effort was to be made to teach their parents too. 'English for Immigrants' campaigns were launched by the DES and implemented by all schools designated multiracial and by the Community Relations Councils for adults in the community. Programmes that aimed to help black students were influenced by the official explanations that black students pose a problem for schools and that this problem needs to be rectified. While the offering of extra tuition in English to black people was indeed most generous, the aim of the teaching programmes were dubious. Within the prevailing education philosophy that portrayed black students negatively, systems of cataloguing were devised to describe the linguistic position of black people. Alleyne for example (in Carby, H., 1982, p. 187) used three categories: total language deficiency, partial language deficiency and dialect impediments. According to these categories, children from the Caribbean, Asia or Africa were considered as having total language deficiency if they could speak their own language but could not read or write in their own or English language. Black children were said to have 'partial language deficiency' if they could speak little English, had a script in their own language or in English and could speak fluently in their own language. Black children were seen to suffer from dialect impediments if they spoke English fluently but in a Caribbean dialect. The language of a group of Caribbean people — Creole — was considered to be the cause of this unfortunate problem. And so, according to the first and second categories, speaking an African or Asian language did not count as having a language at all. Black children speaking their own language were seen as backward, not as bilingual or potentially bilingual.

Institutions such as the National Foundation for Educational Research declared that 'language is one major factor in this culturally induced backwardness of immigrant children and affects assessment of ability and actual school performance (NFER, 1966, p. 173). Thus total assimilation through language was envisaged and black languages were not to survive. The intention was not just to teach young black people English, but also to rectify their alleged cultural backwardness for the purposes of benefiting from the British education system.

The initial multi-racial education policies totally disregarded the history of the political economic relationship between Britain and black people, for they simply aimed to absorb black students into the British schools and society. Having assumed that white middle-class culture is necessary for living in Britain, black cultures, languages and knowledge about black history were seen as inappropriate and unnecessary. The assimilation policies of the Department of Education and Science are a classic example of the institutionalization of a systematic invalidation of an oppressed group's identity and history.

The failure of the assimilation policies within the British education system and society soon became evident. Most black people were simply not prepared to discard their heritage and identity. The small group of black people who accepted the principle of 'When in [the Empire of] Rome . . .' and became British, found that in so doing, their experiences of racism did not diminish. 'During this period black people had to find, and found ways of combatting the terrible and often violent and vicious racism experienced in their everyday lives' (Brandt, G.L., 1986, p. 13). In the sphere of education, black parents organized against the dispersal of their children over vast geographical areas. The dissatisfaction of the black people and the inadequacies of the assimilation policies thus contributed towards the British state adopting what came to be known as the integration strategy within society at large and within its institutions.

The integration approach was a liberal version of the assimilation philosophy. Fundamentally, both the assimilation and integration philosophies are based on the myth that there exists a unity within the British nation with no profound inequalities. Whereas the assimilation policies sought to maintain this mythical unity by expecting everyone to become part of a homogeneous society by discarding all differences, the integration policies offered a longer, more tolerant route. The new version of assimilation policies allowed black people some limited cultural diversity in the areas of religious beliefs, certain customs, dress and language. The final aim was no longer a quick absorption of all groups into the British society, but a more gradual process of assimilation. The rationale of the integration policies was that, if black people are allowed to maintain certain aspects of their culture, they will experience a sense of social security, independence and confidence, all of which will help them to integrate into the British society. Through this process of integration, black people were expected to accept rather than reject the crucial political and economic values that shape the British society (Mullard, 1982, p. 120).

In education, integration was defined by Roy Jenkins as, 'not a flattening process of assimilation but equal opportunity accompanied by cultural diversity in an atmosphere of mutual tolerance' (Mullard, 1982, p. 125). The greater liberal element of the integration policies was evident in their concern about the lack of equality of opportunity in education, particularly regarding the disproportionately large numbers of African and Asian students in 'educationally subnormal' schools. The integration approach for education was outlined in the report from the Select Committee on Race Relations and Immigration, *The Problems of the Coloured School-Leavers* (1969). This report analysed the position of black school leavers, the problems that they experience and, finally, the report outlined the action that needed to be taken.

The Select Committee, like the previous Committees, reinforced British racism. It stated that even though there have been many people from different parts of the world who have chosen to come to work and live in Britain, the problem of the latest influx of immigrants was the 'darker colour of their skin'. The Committee continued to say that although all immigrants should be treated as full and equal citizens, irrespective of the colour of their skin, it is not always easy to do so. We are told that people are 'suspicious' of strangers. They 'fear' competition for their jobs, for the houses for which they have waited a long time, for social resources, schools and hospitals beds. Moreover, people 'feel ill at ease' when mixing with people with different languages, religion, dress or social customs and that these anxieties are 'exacerbated by differences in the colour of people's skin' (Select Committee on Race Relations and Immigration, 1969, p. 5). Having reduced the dynamic of racism to the 'understandable fears' of white people, the members of this Select Committee ignored the historical development and the present day manifestations of racism.

With regards to the education of black students, the Committee offered further insights. In a section entitled, 'Complex of disabilities', we are told that young black people experience problems due to 'cultural shock', lack of contact between schools and parents, poor command of the English language, general deprivation and the widespread lack of understanding of black people in this society. Once the 'disabilities' of black people were outlined, the Committee suggested that 'white people in the host community should try to understand coloured people and immigrants should try to understand the problems of the host people'. The major problem of race relations was considered to be a lack of understanding between the 'host' community and the 'immigrant' community, not legislative, institutional and individual racism. Thus the Committee argued that the educational challenge should be to foster tolerance between black and white people. By pathologizing black students and portraying them as having 'disabilities', the Committee effectively diverted attention from this country's numerous racist structures that impact upon young black people daily.

Next the Select Committee pondered upon the question of equality of opportunities; its recommendations are illuminative. We are told that equality of opportunity does not always mean treating everyone in exactly the same way, that all people are not equal and that 'special problems' need 'special treatment'. The Committee explained carefully that this principle is applied in many areas, for example, economically depressed areas in Britain and overseas get financial assistance, 'backward' school children are given special attention and physically handicapped people are given special assistance in both education and employment (SCRRI, 1969, p. 31). A perspective which pathologizes an oppressed group has its own answers for problems — the Committee suggested that the principal of offering 'special treatment for special problems' should be applied to black students since they are 'handicapped' in competing with other school-leavers (SCRRI, 1969).

Essentially, this 'special treatment' involved being more understanding of black students and their background. The best way of achieving this was to prepare all children for life in a multiracial society. This, the Select Committee argued, can be achieved by teaching about the countries of the black students. It is interesting that 'learning about the countries of black students' did not mean learning about black history. It is suggested that primary school children in Hackney or Brixton could be taught Caribbean songs, and children in Wolverhampton could be shown Indian art, jewellery and costumes. The idea was that this would help bring 'immigrant children into the life of the school' and presumably also reduce white students' 'fears' of black people (SCRRI, 1969, p. 41).

While this Select Committee recommended that black students should be included in school life through the exposition of black songs, art, jewellery and costumes, it also stressed that black students ought to be sufficiently socialized into the British way of life. Teachers were told that 'Deliberate efforts should be made to teach newly arrived immigrants about life in this country — our customs, sports conventions and industrial activities as well as our language' (SCRRI, 1969, p. 42).

It is clear, therefore, that the Select Committee on Race Relations and Immigration perceived black people in a particular way, analysed the position of black students accordingly and made recommendations which were in line with the original perceptions. Black people were seen to have strange customs and habits. The racism of white people was considered to be a reasonable fear of strangers with dark skins. Black students were considered to have complex disabilities and needed treatment accordingly. Finally, the Committee urged schools to play a leading role in the development of greater awareness of black people through the appreciation of black costumes, songs and jewellery while not forgetting British customs and conventions. Herein lay the racism and tokenism of the Select Committee and the integration policies that it constructed. According to the Select Committee on Race Relations and Immigration, the history of black people and their political economic relationship with Britain were considered insignificant for the development of an understanding about black people in Britain's education institutions.

Policies that treat people with a lack of respect cannot expect to succeed.

The integration policies failed miserably. Besides the rhetoric of equality of opportunities for black people, there was little positive change in the position of black students. The challenge from the black communities therefore gained a greater momentum. In particular, the African community resisted strongly the explanations being offered to them regarding the 'poor performance' of their children in schools. In response to this resistance, a new committee chaired by A. Rampton was set up by the Government in 1979. The aim of this committee was to examine education needs of racial minority students in the school system. This committee produced a report called *Education of Children from Ethnic Minority Groups* (DES, 1981).

The Rampton Committee appeared to herald a shift in the analysis of the position of black students, for it began by mentioning that racism is a major factor which contributes towards black students not succeeding in the education system. However, the Committee's lengthy report offered very little information on racism. The few paragraphs on this subject associated racism with people's attitudes alone. Within education, racism was seen in terms of misinformed teachers' 'unintentional' negative attitudes and behaviour towards black students (DES, 1981, p. 12).

The words 'racism' and 'institutional racism' were carefully scattered in the first few pages of the report, and the Committee explained that 'traditional educational practices, originally established to cater for the needs of a generally homogeneous population, can, in fact, operate in discriminatory ways when applied to today's society' (DES, 1981, p. 14). Institutional racism, according to this Committee, therefore, is the manner in which a once fair and just education system now responds negatively towards black students. The Committee did not acknowledge that the British education system has a long history of discrimination against women and working-class students. Gender and class conflicts were ignored as the British public were lumped together as a homogeneous group. By stating that the education system has only recently (after the influx of black people) begun to operate in discriminatory ways, a suggestion was made by the Committee that if there were no black people in Britain, the education system would have continued to be a fair one, catering for a white homogeneous population. Thus, once again we see that the dialectical analysis of the history of racism is not considered. And, again we see that racism is not viewed as a live and dynamic ideology which legitimizes racial inequalities at all levels of this society.

Previously, the Select Committee on Race Relations and Immigration had urged black and white people to be more tolerant of each other and suggested that schools ought to play an active role in this process. The Rampton Committee's Report was essentially an elaboration of this message. While the Select Committee urged black and white people to be more understanding towards each other in order to help black people feel at ease and integrate into this society (once black people had been appropriately socialized), the Rampton Committee encouraged a greater celebration of black peoples' cultures.

According to the Rampton Committee, Britain is a culturally diverse country, and a good education cannot be based on one culture alone. We are told that education should not 'seek to iron out the differences between cultures, nor attempt to draw everyone into the dominant culture'. Education should 'draw upon the experiences of the many cultures that make up our society and thus broaden the cultural horizons of every child' thereby offering every child a 'multicultural education' (DES, 1981, pp. 26–27).

Essentially, multicultural education, according to the Rampton Committee, involved learning about certain elements of different cultures, for example, religious festivals, diets and cooking habits, fashion and music of minority groups. Culture was viewed as an apolitical entity. Learning about different cultures was not considered in terms of examining the process by which different cultures have been and are produced in relations of power, or how certain cultures are produced through violence, domination and exploitation, and others are produced through struggle and resistance. A historical understanding of the unequal position held by black people in this society and its education institution was thus replaced by a superficial acknowledgment of the cultures of black people living in Britain.

It is significant that the Rampton Committee was pleased to explain that, at a time of constraints on public spending, most of their recommendations would require no additional expenditure (DES, 1981, p. 85). The most important aim of multicultural education was for teachers to 'play a leading role in seeking to bring about a change in attitudes on the part of the society as a whole towards ethnic minority groups' (DES, 1981, p. 14).

In the event of extra staff being employed, for example, multicultural advisers, the Committee did not recommend any new sources of funding, it simply reinforced two already established avenues. These were the 75 per cent grants made by the central government for the employment of extra staff under the Section 11 of the Local Government Act of 1966 and second, grants given under the Urban Programmes to areas of 'special need' which include work with black people.

The Rampton Committee also recommended that education authorities should have a clear statement of policy objectives on education for a multicultural society with guidance for all schools on how to implement the policy. Furthermore, the Committee put forward many recommendations, ranging from curriculum development to the role of the DES in combatting racism. The multicultural framework for change that the Rampton Committee offered did not include the examination of the historical development of oppression and underdevelopment. Hence the strategies in 'combatting racism' and curriculum development, even for subjects such as history, involved learning about only some elements of the cultures of black people.

The multicultural education policy is clearly not as crude as the assimilation or integration policies. However, despite the Rampton Committee's condemnation of racism (narrowly defined as unintentional negative attitudes and behaviour towards black people), the multicultural model which it advocated shares the same long-term aim as the other two models, that is, the maintenance of an unequal society. Unlike the other Committees, the Rampton Committee realized that a total denial of black people's identity would eventually result in rebellion by black people. Thus, the Rampton Committee recommended an approach which on the surface appeared to offer black people more than had been offered by the other Committees.

After the interim report of the Rampton Committee, Lord Swann was asked to take the chairmanship of the final report, *Education for All* (DES, 1985). The Swann report (DES, 1985) consolidated the multicultural model advocated by the Rampton Committee and named it 'cultural pluralist education for all'.

The Swann report is a lengthy piece of work containing 807 pages and covering most aspects of schooling ranging from the hidden curriculum and teaching materials to the external examination boards and the DES. It is clear that the production of the report has required a great deal of work and resources, and numerous people from within the school system and the community have made contributions.

In its initial analysis, the report stressed that racism, social, and economic forces are all factors that contribute towards the underachievement of black students in British schools. The report even explained that the disadvantaged social and economic position that black people hold in this society is the result of 'racial prejudice and discrimination, especially in the areas of employment and housing' (DES, 1985, p. 89). However, with regards to concrete recommendations, the Swann Committee followed in the footsteps of its predecessor and argued that most of the recommendations would mainly involve 'psychological' expenditure (DES, 1985, p. 767).

The report makes a strong case for a 'pluralist' (previously called multicultural) education for all, which involves enabling all students to understand and accept the multicultural nature of British society. Although the Committee acknowledged that racism and socio-economic factors affect the performance of black students in schools, in its recommendations, teachers are urged simply to encourage students to learn about the different cultures that exist in Britain today.

Like its predecessor, the Swann Committee argued that a greater awareness of black cultures will lead to better race relations and reduce racial prejudice and discrimination. This Committee also had a narrow perspective on black cultures and focused on safe and exotic areas, for example, fashion, cuisine, music and dance. The emphasis was on the cultural 'characteristics' of the constituent minority groups (Africans, Indians, Pakistanis, Chinese, Travellers, Muslims, Vietnamese), not on the common historical and present day experiences of the exploited groups. Subjects such as history, political education and geography are thus discussed within a framework which disregards the need to study Britain's political economy of racism (DES, 1985, p. 234 and pp. 340 to 343).

While one does not wish to cynically dismiss any positive anti-racist efforts, it is important to see the limitations of what is being offered in the interest of black people. The Rampton and Swann Committees did not treat black people with contempt, for they did not totally dismiss black people's roots and traditions. They argued that black people have an interesting culture and that if only white people could get to know black people better, white people could then begin to like black people and not be nasty to them. If white people are kinder to people who have dark skins, then black people will feel more comfortable in this country and join in the British way of life.

Such simplistic analysis of racism is not only inadequate, it is dangerous. In the long term, the multicultural or cultural pluralist model for education, as advocated by the two Committees, masks the problem of racism and weakens the struggle against it. The multicultural/cultural pluralist model for education disregards black history and advocates a superficial debate on culture.

Many people do argue that greater cultural awareness is at least a beginning, but the question is, where does it lead us? Brandt explains that

> Racism in education is very complex and far reaching in its impact and ultimate effects. Thus the deconstruction of institutional racist practices must be direct and at a conscious level. It is dangerous if not downright racist to concentrate on something else, like culture for example, and hope that the rest will follow and racism will end. (Brandt, 1986, p. 71)

The last chapter argued that the disregard for the creative history of black people and the history of the political economic relationship between Britain and black people has legitimized racism and continues to contribute towards the oppression of black people today. Historically, the denial of the history and the identity of black people was an important strategy used by the British and other Europeans to enslave and colonize black people.

This chapter has illustrated that the British state, through various Committees, has planned numerous strategies for the assimilation of black students into the British education system and society at large. This has been attempted through the implementation of policies based on various education models: the blunt assimilation model, the less crude integration model and the liberal multicultural/cultural pluralist model. None of these models offer a genuine respect for the identity and history of black people. At most, black people are viewed as having quaint and exotic cultures. The denial of black history continues.

In 1979, Verma and Bagley convincingly illustrated that black students are 'sentenced to mediocrity' within the British education system (Verma and Bagley, 1979). Today, this situation has changed little (See Troyna and Carrington, 1990). So, within the black community there is a growing feeling of discontent and a desire for 'a total withdrawal from the schooling of the state because that schooling is by definition racist and, thus, a major tool for the genocide of black people' (Brandt, 1986, p. 108). Other sections of the black community continue to struggle from within the education system without losing sight of the fact that for several centuries British racism has been nurtured both within the educational establishments and in society at large. This position considers the education system to be a valuable site for struggle and seizes every opportunity for oppositional action.

The next chapter is for teachers who are struggling within the school system to find ways of helping their students to make sense of the world in which they live without reinforcing the oppressive forces in the society at large or in the education system. Chapter 4 outlines how, through the study of history, teachers can offer their students the opportunity to learn about the history of domination, oppression and resistance, thereby enabling students to understand and challenge exploitation and to live constructively.

Chapter 4

Liberating the National History Curriculum

Racism in education will not end simply because black students and their white counterparts have studied 'ethnic' cuisine, jewellery and costumes. The struggle against racism begins by understanding the history of racism for, 'it is impossible to bring about a deliberate and purposeful change in the present without knowing how this present state came about' (Szentes, T., 1971, p. 17).

Over the last three decades, various governments have requested special committees to examine the needs of black students and to suggest strategies for improving the position of minority groups in the education system. Chapter 3 demonstrated that none of the government sponsored committees have recommended teaching students about the history of British racism.

The Schools Council Project, 'History 13–16', was set up in 1972. This pivotal project marked a major turning point in the teaching of history. The Schools Council Project (1976) embodied a new approach which challenged the more traditional history teaching methods of mastering 'factual' material. The Schools Council Project aimed to encourage students not to be mere recipients of a body of information but to develop investigative skills in order to make sense of the past. The 'new' history's emphasis on the *process* rather than on the *content*, however, resulted in the exclusion of certain areas of history. Conceived at a time when black people were being encouraged to discard their identity and assimilate into the British society, this radical history teaching project failed to integrate black history into its curriculum.

The British government has recently introduced a National Curriculum for most subjects including history (DES, 1991). The National History Curriculum (England and Wales) includes both the traditional and the Schools Council's 'new history' teaching approaches. Fortunately, the National History Curriculum allows teachers to develop their own teaching materials, so teachers do not have to offer their students a basic concoction of the traditional and the new history. Thus, in spite of the British State's efforts to control what the next generation will learn and know, teachers could if they wish, (with creative planning), offer their students a liberating history based on the historical experiences of the majority of people, that is, a people's history.

A people's history would aim to examine how groups of people lived in the past and related to each other. A study of a people's history with a liberating perspective would attempt to include the perspective of the political economic base that existed between groups of people, thereby making sense of their social and cultural lifestyles. Such a history would acknowledge the grandeur of the costumes and the court life of kings and queens, but it would not necessarily dwell upon these elements unduly. A study of a people's history would focus on the power exercised and maintained by kings and queens in relation to the people that they ruled.

Learning just the stories about some heroines that lived in the past is not a study of a people's history from a liberating perspective, for such a study requires an investigation of the causes and the nature of the oppression experienced by women through the ages. A study of a people's history does not focus primarily on the creativity of a small group of people when examining the development of their country. With regards to the development of Britain for example, a study of a people's history would not simply involve learning about the famous British men who invented great machines that supposedly revolutionized agricultural and industrial production in Britain. A study of a people's history from a liberating perspective would indeed acknowledge the British inventive geniuses, but it would also examine the contribution of the British workers, the African slaves and the workers of the British colonies towards Britain's industrial revolution.

A study of a people's history from a liberating perspective is not the same as learning about isolated, unrelated incidents of the past, for such a study requires a critical exploration of the continuous and everchanging relationships between groups of people within the context of their political, economic, social and cultural lives. A study of a people's history is not made up of investigating discrete events of the past, but it involves a rigorous examination of the dialectical nature of historical development and underdevelopment, of power and exploitation, of oppression and resistance in order to make some sense of past and present experiences of groups of people.

The National History Curriculum is seen by some as 'thrusting Christianity into "a position of embarrassing prominence"', and as making demands for a 'more Anglocentric, patriotic approach to history teaching' (Troyna and Carrington, 1990, p. 102). If this is so, what hope is there for teachers to offer their students opportunities to explore and learn about the history of black people?

This chapter illustrates with the example of the National History Curriculum (England) how teachers can liberate the National History Curriculum and encourage students to learn not only about the history of racism but also about the history of sexism and class oppression. In this way the history of black people is not compartmentalized but is situated within the context of a people's history. The aim is not to be divisive but to seek a unity for the future by understanding and accepting the positive and the negative of our collective past. The next chapter (5), gives examples of history lesson plans which aim to weave a people's history into the National History Curriculum.

The official aim of the National History Curriculum is to ensure that the young people of this country learn about the history of Britain. The National Curriculum History Working Group confirms this:

> An understanding of British history should be the foundation of pupils' historical learning, since it is the main framework of their immediate experience, in political, economic, social and cultural terms. (DES, 1990, p. 16)

That young people in British schools should learn about the history of Britain is not being disputed here. The question that is being asked is, what aspects of Britain's history should they be taught? Historically Britain has been a powerful country. Should the next generation be taught about the greatness of Britain's past, or should they be taught about how Britain became 'Great'? When studying the history of 'Great' Britain, the contribution of the British women, men and children labourers and the peoples of the former British Empire cannot be ignored.

One of the aims of teaching history in schools, according to the History National Curriculum, is to help students to understand the present in the context of the past: 'There is nothing in the present that cannot be better understood in the light of its historical context and origins'. Another aim is to prepare pupils for adult life. We are told that

> history gives pupils a framework of reference, opportunities for the informed use of leisure, and a critically sharpened intelligence with which to make sense of current affairs. History is a priceless preparation for citizenship, work and leisure. It encourages pupils to approach them from angles not considered by other subjects or forms of study in the curriculum. (DES, 1990, pp. 1–2)

If the aim of history is to help students to make sense of the past in order to understand the present and to respond to the future constructively, then the history that they are taught should not be based primarily on the selected glories of the past. Making sense of the present from half-truths about the past is not possible. With a distorted understanding about the present, it is not possible to participate fully in society. Teachers may therefore wish to find ways of teaching a British history which does not only focus on the greatness of Britain's past but a history which examines how this development was achieved.

When planning the history programmes, it is most important that teachers and parents realize that the National History Curriculum is aimed at being accessible to teachers and is therefore briefer and less prescriptive than the original proposals of the History Working Group. The National Curriculum Council states: 'Without loss of rigour, the study units are now briefer and give teachers greater discretion to select appropriate content' (National Curriculum Council, 1990b, letter to the Secretary of State for Education and Science). Teachers need not follow the step-by-step programmes offered by the History Working Group (DES, 1990) or the Non-Statutory Guidance produced by the National Curriculum Council (1991), since these programmes are not part of the statutory instruments of the History National Curriculum Attainment Targets and Programmes of Study Order of 1991 (DES, 1991).

Parents and teachers may wish to seize opportunities for offering the next generation a broad understanding of British history. To do this, teachers need to be imaginative in the planning of their teaching programmes rather than following uncritically the recommendations of the government. Parents need to be vigilant in their observations of what their children are being taught in the name of British history and must challenge head teachers if they are not satisfied.

When preparing a people's history one question that comes to mind is, at what age are children ready to understand such a history? For example, teaching young children about a queen or a king is indeed easier than helping them to explore the historical factors which contributed towards the hardships endured by the peasants. Nonetheless, if it is believed that students ought to learn about the history of the majority of people, then imaginative ways of making a people's history accessible to young children as well as to adolescents need to be developed. Since the History National Curriculum is the framework within which teachers are being asked to operate, teachers need to find ways of offering a people's history within the boundaries imposed upon them. The National Curriculum requires schools to begin teaching history to children from the age of five years onwards. It is suggested that 'pupils should be given opportunities to develop an awareness of the past and of the ways in which it was different from the present' (DES, 1991, p. 13). The programme of study for five to seven-year-old children consists of one study unit which has to be taught throughout the key stage. The teacher could quite legitimately include in this key stage elements of the history of the white working-class people, black people, and the specific experiences and contribution of women to history. These elements of history could be pursued in relation to the National Curriculum's recommendation that

Pupils should be helped to develop an awareness of the past through stories from different periods and cultures including:
1   well-known myths and legends;
2   stories about historical events;
3   eyewitness accounts of historical events;
4   fictional stories set in the past. (DES, 1991, p. 13)

The section on well-known myths and legends, for example, could include myths and prejudices about people that are poor, black people, women, disabled people and other minority groups. Most children are aware that British society is composed of white as well as black people. Teachers could include legends and stories about historical events from Britain as well as from the countries of origins of black children (AFFOR, 1983).

For Key Stage One as with the other key stages, the National Curriculum offers useful recommendations for making history lessons interesting for students and suggests that pupils should have the opportunity to learn about the past from a range of historical sources, including artefacts, pictures and photographs, music, adults talking about their own past, written sources, buildings and sites. While this is a very positive recommendation, the National History Curriculum has serious flaws. It excludes the examination of the dialectical nature of historical development, particularly in relation to Britain's development. Britain's development through the slave trade and colonialism, for example, is either skimmed over or ignored. This chapter will now look at some of these gaps in the National Curriculum and offer suggestions as to how these gaps can be filled.

While the first key stage comprises only one compulsory unit, the second and the third key stages are composed of core study units and supplementary study units. (See Appendix 1 and 2 for an example of a core unit and a supplementary unit prescribed by the National Curriculum.) Since the National History Curriculum as yet does not include word-by-word lesson plans for schools to follow, teachers may wish to exercise their freedom by choosing their own content as much as possible within the broad outline of the National Curriculum.

Key Stage Two is for eight to eleven-year-old students. It covers twelve terms over a period of four years. The National History Curriculum recommends:

> Pupils should be taught about important episodes and developments in Britain's past, from Roman to modern times. They should have opportunities to investigate local history. They should be taught about ancient civilisations and the history of other parts of the world. They should be helped to develop a sense of chronology and to learn about changes in everyday life over long periods of time. (DES, 1991, p. 15)

This key stage consists of nine study units and teachers have a choice of selecting either five or six core study units followed by either three or four supplementary units. The core study units include:

1   Invaders and settlers: Romans, Anglo-Saxons, and Vikings in Britain;
2   Tudor and Stuart times;
3   Victorian Britain;
4   Britain since 1930;

5   Ancient Greece;
6   Exploration and encounters 1450 to 1550.

The concepts and terminology used by the National History Curriculum in the outline of the core study unit, 'Invaders and settlers: Romans, Anglo-Saxons and Vikings in Britain' are interesting. Examples include: 'raids', 'invasions', 'settlements' and 'resistance'. In the next core unit, 'Tudor and Stuart times', one section looks at the beginning of the British Empire. Here, the words raids, invasions, settlements and resistance to British rule are excluded. Instead, the emphasis is on the explorations of the heroes who dared to voyage across the mighty oceans; pirates such as Drake and Raleigh are also considered significant. The National Curriculum does not mention how the British and other European explorers of this period set the doors open to massive raids, invasions and settlements, and how, in fact, there was a formidable resistance against European expansion overseas even during this early stage of empire building. Nevertheless, there is no reason why teachers cannot elaborate on this aspect of British history; after all, the provision of the National History Curriculum does allow teachers to have discretion to select their own content. In this way, teachers can ensure that the history that they offer to their students is not a perpetuation of an Eurocentric history.

Although the National Curriculum does not mention the progressive groups of this period, teachers may still wish to include them in the section entitled, 'The way of life of different groups in town and country' in the second core study unit of Key Stage Two. During the Tudor and the Stuart times, groups such as the Diggers, the Ranters, the Levellers and others challenged the relations between the rich and the poor in England and demanded the establishment of communal property for all (Hill, 1972). In contrast to the Diggers, the Ranters and the Levellers, other groups of this time, for example, the land owners, the clergy and the factory owners could also be studied for the role that they played in the time of the Tudor, Stuart and subsequent monarchs. Besides the class differences in Britain during this period, there were also marked differences between the position of women and men. In this section dealing with the way of life of different groups during the Tudor and the Stuart times, teachers may wish to explore with the students the role of women and men from different classes of people (Hill, 1972).

The third core study unit, 'Victorian Britain', aims to introduce students to:

... life in Victorian Britain and its legacy to the present day. The focus should be on men, women and children at different levels of society in different areas of Victorian England, Wales, Scotland and Ireland and on how they were affected by industrialisation. (DES, 1991, p. 23)

This unit offers many possibilities for teachers to include the history of the working-class people in Victorian Britain. The history of the life experiences of children, women and men of Britain in different classes during the Victorian era could be included under the section, 'Victorian families'. Unlike the children of the rich, the children of the poor had limited educational and vocational opportunities as they struggled in the mills for long hours. The oppression of women of different classes also took different forms. While the middle-class women were restricted to life within the boundaries of their (wealthy) homes, the working-class women struggled in their own homes and as domestic servants in homes of the rich or in the mines and the factories. In contrast to the wealthy men, the life opportunities for the unemployed and the working-class men were also greatly reduced by the hardships imposed upon them through their employment or unemployment (Thompson, 1963).

Britain's Victorian imperial history is entitled, 'Trade and the growth of the British Empire' in this unit, and it could quite easily reinforce the idea that the development of the British Empire was a result of Britain's trade with people who unfortunately were not advanced enough to govern themselves in a civilized manner. The growth of the British Empire was not simply an outcome of trade. The National Curriculum does not consider it necessary to mention Britain's 'one way trade' with other countries during the Victorian era. Nevertheless, because teachers are allowed to select their own teaching materials, they may wish to encourage students to explore the true essence of the British Empire's trade with other countries (Mukherjee, 1974; Rodney, 1972). This could be done by examining the British people's and the colonized people's perspective of trade during the days of the British Empire. Teachers would thus offer their students a valuable lesson by showing that history is recorded with numerous perspectives — thereby meeting the requirement of Attainment Target 2, 'Interpretations of history'.

Besides 'Trade and growth of the British Empire', the National Curriculum recommends that students be taught about the inventions and scientific discoveries of this period. In order not to limit the scope to a Eurocentric perspective, teachers may wish to find ways of including a study of scientific, medical, astrological, mathematical and other inventions of not only European countries but countries such as Africa, China, Arabia, India as well (Shan and Bailey, 1991; Cotterell, 1980). In this way students would learn to value the creativity of all people.

The fourth core unit of Key Stage Two is 'Britain since 1930', and it includes, among other topics, 'changes in the role of men and women and in the family'. Here is a challenge for teachers not to reproduce, out of convenience, the basic sociology text about 'the family'. Although it is necessary to examine the greater choices available to women (especially in certain classes) in this century compared to the last, it is also important to examine the continued inequalities experienced by women. Prejudices that students might have about the position of women and men in the family and in society could also be discussed, and teachers may wish to offer the students a women's perspective for making sense of the inequalities experienced by women through history (Bird, *et al.*, 1979; Bilton, *et al.*, 1981).

Any discussion on the changes in the family through history cannot ignore the intervention of the British government in this important and personal area of life. The state has been attempting to perpetuate only some family models, although numerous family structures have existed in this country throughout history and have continued to survive.

Clause 28 of the Local Government Act 1986 (prohibition of political publicity) has resulted in many teachers ignoring discussions about lesbians and gays even though a significant number of people are not heterosexual, and many lesbians and gay men do have children in schools (Kent-Baguley, 1988). Indeed Section 28 of the Local Government Act 1986 does state that

1 A local authority shall not;
    a) intentionally promote homosexuality or publish material with the intention of promoting homosexuality;
    b) promote the teaching in any maintained school of the acceptability of homosexuality as pretended family relationship.
2 Nothing in subsection 1 above shall be taken to prohibit the doing of anything for the purpose of treating or preventing the spread of disease.

However, teachers also need to realize that the National Curriculum Guidance 5 — Health Education states that pupils should:

... be aware of the range of sexual attitudes and behaviours in present day society,

... be aware that feeling positive about sexuality and sexual activity is important in relationships ... (National Curriculum Council, 1990a, p. 6).

Myths about homosexuals as 'perverts' and ideas about 'proper' families consisting of a mother, father, and two children (where the father goes out to earn a living and the mother cares for the children and the home) are encouraged in this society, and they abound even among the young members of our society. If a group of students raise questions about family structures, teachers may wish to encourage them to explore the range of family units that exist in this society today (and have existed in British and other societies of this world throughout history). Students would then learn that not all 'couples' are made up of a man and a woman and that people not living in a 'proper' families are not 'pretending' at being a family (Jeffs and Smith, 1990; Allen, 1987; Harris, 1990). The aim of this would be to help students to have a perspective about society that is rooted in reality rather than on unfounded notions about how people live. Such an exploration of family systems through history could be included in this key stage's section entitled 'Changes in the role of men and women and in family life'.

The section on 'Immigration and emigration' in this unit could be developed by teachers into an opportunity for students to learn about the centuries of global emigration of the British people to the numerous countries of its empire, as well as the immigration of the Irish people, the European Jewish people and the black people of the ex-British colonies to Britain. Exploring the causes of emigration and immigration could help students to gain an insight into the complex forces which have driven people to leave their homelands. Such an exercise would also challenge the widely held myth that all immigrants who have come to Britain are black and that they have come to 'scrounge' from its welfare state. Situating the dynamics of this country's migration patterns within the dialectical relationship between Britain and the countries it colonized is useful for this purpose (Tierney, 1982).

Core Study Unit Five examines the ancient civilization of Greece and its 'legacy to the modern world'. In this unit, as in the rest of the History Curriculum, the National History Curriculum's historical perspective is significant. In the statutory guidelines, there is no mention of the contribution of the African and the Asian ancient civilizations to the civilization of Greece. Should teachers strictly follow the outline offered by the National Curriculum, thereby giving students a Eurocentric view of ancient civilizations, or should they attempt to offer a non-Eurocentric history of this world's ancient civilizations?

An interesting aspect of the history of ancient civilizations is their relationship between each other. There is growing evidence that the civilizations of Egypt and Western Asia made a major contribution towards the civilizations of ancient Greece and Rome (Bernal, 1987). However, this link has been ignored over the centuries as European historians have worked towards perpetuating the myth that the Graeco-Roman tradition is European and pure white. Teachers may wish to encourage their students to examine the popular European myth that democracy and philosophy are rooted exclusively in ancient European civilizations. This could be done by offering students opportunities to research, not only the Greek and Roman civilizations, but other ancient civilizations of the world, too. In this way students could gain an insight into how all the ancient civilizations have left legacies to this world.

The final Core Study Unit, Number Six, of the second key stage is 'Exploration and encounters 1450 to 1550'. The National Curriculum suggests:

> Pupils should be introduced to the developments which brought Europeans into contact with American peoples. The focus should be on the reasons for the voyages of exploration, the Spanish voyages, the nature of Aztec civilisation, the encounter between the two cultures and its results. (DES, 1991, p. 29)

It is interesting that when the designers of the National Curriculum consider the history of other countries, they do so with an accuracy that they do not manage with the history of Britain. This key stage deals with the period 1450 to 1550 when the Spanish and the Portuguese were the leading European explorers. Whereas earlier, the National Curriculum dealt with the issue of the British Empire in terms of examining the 'trade' between Britain and other countries, in this unit, the examination of the Spanish empire is quite different. There is space given to the study of the people who were colonized through a study of the Aztec civilization. The focus on the 'Spanish conquest' avoids any reinforcement of the myth that empire building was a benevolent outcome of some 'trading' links. Why does the National Curriculum not encourage teachers to use a similar perspective when teaching about the imperial history of Britain?

Within Key Stage Two, teachers may choose either three or four supplementary units from three categories. The first category is a study of a theme over a long period of time, chosen from:

1 Ships and seafarers;
2 Food and farming;
3 Houses and places of worship;
4 Writing and printing;
5 Land transport;
6 Domestic life, families and childhood. (DES, 1991, p. 31)

The National Curriculum recommends that this unit should

— involve the study of important historical issues;
— cover a time span of at least 1000 years;
— compare developments in different periods;
— show links between local, British, European and world history. (DES, 1991, p. 31)

In the section entitled 'Ships and seafarers' teachers may wish to offer students opportunities to explore information about the ships that Africans, Asians, South Americans and the Chinese built and sailed in hundreds of years ago (Cotterell, 1980), thereby not reinforcing the myth that ships were first built by Europeans and that non-European people were less advanced seafarers. Teachers could also quite legitimately include in this unit a study of the ships that were used for the transportation of African slaves and Indian indentured labourers (Rodney, 1970; Tinker, 1974). In this way, teachers would avoid reinforcing the notion that the magnificent ships in which the Europeans first sailed the oceans were simply used for 'discovering' dark and mysterious continents.

For the section on 'Food and farming through history' teachers may choose to offer students opportunities to learn about various systems of farming that Britain has developed through history, for example:

1 Sugar cane farming on the slave plantations in the Caribbean in the eighteenth century, (Reynolds, 1985);
2 The highland clearances and sheep farming in Scotland in the nineteenth century, (Prebble, 1963);
3 Cash crop farming in the British colonies in Africa in the twentieth century. (Rodney, 1972)

Teachers could help students explore how and why the above agricultural systems came into being, and who benefited from the products of the three systems. In order not to give the impression that the workers of these systems were docile recipients of the order imposed upon them, teachers could offer information about the various forms of resistance that the farming families in Scotland, the Caribbean and other British colonies mounted during the 'agricultural revolutions' and after in Britain and abroad.

The section on 'Domestic life, families and childhood' could be developed into a most interesting study of family life in a range of settings. Taking the National Curriculum's recommendation that this unit ought to show links between national and international history, the teacher may want to choose the following settings to explore family life with students:

1 Feudal Britain, (Houlbrooke, 1984);
2 Britain's slave plantation colonies, (Bryan *et al.*, 1985);
3 Britain's indentured labour colonies. (Tinker, 1974)

To ensure that students do not view family life in isolation, teachers may wish to encourage students to explore the socio-economic organization of feudal, slave and indentured labour systems within which families were situated. The power relation between the beneficiaries and the workers of the systems was an important aspect of these organizations. The unequal positions held by children, women and men within each of the above settings were also a significant aspect of family life.

So far, we have seen that teachers can, if they so wish, structure their lesson plans in such a way that they legitimately weave a people's history into the National Curriculum. The other supplementary units of Key Stage Two on local history and a past non-European society could also be developed in such a way.

Key Stage Three is for twelve- to fourteen-year-old students for a period of nine terms over three years. This key stage includes four core units and four supplementary units. The recommendation is:

Pupils should be taught to understand how developments from the early Middle Ages to the beginning of the twentieth century helped shape the economy, society, culture and political structure of modern Britain. They should have opportunities to study developments in Europe and the non-European world, and be helped to understand how the histories of different countries are linked. They should be taught about ancient Rome and its legacy to Britain, Europe and the world. (DES, 1991, p. 33)

The four core study units are:

1   The Roman Empire;
2   Medieval realms: Britain, 1066 to 1500;
3   The making of the United Kingdom: Crown, Parliament and people, 1500 to 1750;
4   Expansion, trade and industry: Britain, 1750 to 1900. (DES, 1991, p. 33)

In the study unit, 'Medieval realms; 1066 to 1500', the focus is on topics such as the development of the English monarchy, the feudal society, the legacy of the medieval culture and Christianity as a uniting force within Europe. Beside the popular elements of the history of this period which British history students are always taught — the Norman conquest and the Battle of Hastings (1066); the medieval monarchy and its relationship with the Church barons and the people; the Magna Carta (1215), the Peasants Revolt (1381) and the origins of Parliament; the National Curriculum also recommends that students be taught about the relations between England, Ireland, Scotland and Wales. Here is an opportunity for students to explore the expansion of England into Scotland and Wales and the colonization of Ireland. These historic processes were significant in that they laid the foundations for future overseas expansion and colonization and affected millions of people in Britain and overseas (Worsley, 1984).

The third unit in this key stage is 'The making of the United Kingdom; Crown, Parliament and People, 1500 to 1750'. The National Curriculum for History expects that:

Pupils should be taught about the major political, social and religious changes which shaped the history of Britain during this period. The main focus should be on two themes: the political unification of Britain and the changing relationships between Crown, Parliament and people. (DES, 1991, p. 41)

A significant part of Britain's history during the period covered by this study unit was the building of the British Empire, yet this is not even included in this unit. Why do the designers of the National Curriculum not consider it of importance to study the exploitation of the labour and the wealth of the British colonies for the purposes of building Great Britain? Another important avenue for wealth for Britain during this period was the slave trade. Again, the National Curriculum offers students almost no opportunity to learn about this element of British history. Teachers may wish not to ignore the momentous role that Britain played in the trading of human beings and the colonizing of vast areas of this world. The challenge for teachers is, therefore, to find ways of including the contributions of African and other colonized people towards the building of this country between 1500 and 1750.

Core Unit Four of Key Stage Three is supposed to examine Britain's 'Expansion, trade and industry: 1750 to 1900'. It is recommended that:

> Pupils should be taught about the impact on Britain of industrialisation and world-wide expansion. The focus should be on the growth of trade and industry, the consequences of this for the British Empire and British society, and efforts to make Parliament more responsive to the demands of new social groups. Reference should be made to the histories of England, Ireland, Scotland and Wales. (DES, 1991, p. 43)

Once again we see an attempt to obliterate certain histories from the minds of the younger generation in our society. Rather than acknowledging Britain's imperial role, with all its consequences for the people of Britain's Empire, the National Curriculum expects teachers to focus on certain non-threatening elements of the British history of this period. Rather than accepting that Britain's expansion and development has resulted in the destruction of numerous economies and the underdevelopment of many countries, the British government expects teachers to reproduce the myth that Britain's development was as a result of the great industrial revolution and a world-wide expansion that had a civilizing and a benevolent mission. Generations of British children and the children of its empire have been brought up on such a history. The challenge for teachers, once again, is to find ways of teaching a non-Eurocentric history within the boundaries imposed by the National Curriculum.

With the example of Key Stage Two earlier, we have seen that supplementary units are a good opportunity for teachers to design their own teaching programmes. If teachers wish to offer students a non-Eurocentric and non-sexist view of history, then, with creative planning, it is possible to do so for the National History Curriculum is only a brief outline of subject areas recommended by the state. As yet there are no detailed statutory teaching programmes enforceable by law. Teachers may wish to develop the supplementary units for Key Stage Three as suggested for Key Stage Two.

Key Stage Four is for fifteen to sixteen-year-old students and covers a period of five terms over two years. There are two models that students can follow during this key stage. Model 2 has been designed for those students who wish to follow a full course in history leading to GCSE or equivalent qualification, and Model 1 has been designed for students who wish to follow a short course in history. Model 1 is composed of one core unit and Model 2 comprises the same core unit with an addition of two supplementary units. For Model 1 with no supplementary units, teachers will have to use even greater imagination in order to work within the framework outlined by the National History Curriculum and still offer students a people's history. For Key Stage Four, the National Curriculum recommends that:

> Pupils should be taught to understand how the world in which they live has been shaped by developments in twentieth-century history. This programme of study should develop historical knowledge which will help pupils to understand the background to the modern world, but it is not a course in current affairs. It should focus on events from the turn of the century to about twenty years before the present day. Pupils should be helped to consolidate their understanding of earlier periods of history. Through their historical studies, they should have the opportunities to prepare themselves for citizenship, work and leisure. (DES, 1991, p. 49)

The core unit is entitled 'Britain, Europe and the world in the twentieth century'. The National Curriculum expects that:

> Pupils should be taught about themes in twentieth-century history necessary for them to understand their place and that of Britain in the modern world, in particular:
> — the development of British democracy;
> — international conflict and co-operation, including the Second World War and its impact;
> — economic social and cultural change in Britain and the world.
> (DES, 1991, p. 51)

In studying these themes, the National Curriculum expects pupils to have opportunities to develop awareness of how the histories of Britain, Europe and the world are linked. The statutory outline offered to teachers for covering the above area is brief. Teachers may wish to enable students to have an opportunity to develop a critical perspective of British history. The aim of such a perspective is not to induce guilt in the students as many fear, but to help students to understand and accept the beauty of their history as well as their history's warts. The beauty of British history is the struggle of people in Britain and its colonies for justice, the warts of British history are the destructive and oppressive systems that Britain imposed on its own poor and the peoples of its empire for capital gain.

To help students develop a critical perspective of history, teachers will need to cover areas of history that the designers of the National Curriculum probably did not expect teachers to include in their teaching programmes. Nevertheless, since teachers are being given some opportunities to develop their own teaching materials and since the teaching programmes are not being imposed by the state verbatim, there is no reason why topics such as the ones listed below should not be included.

1 Britain's Role in the Scramble for Africa at the Turn of this Century

The aim of this topic would be to study the relationship between Britain and Africa at the turn of the century. This historical relationship has had and continues to have, enormous consequences for both Africa and Britain. This topic could cover the colonial partitioning and sharing of Africa among the European empire-building powers: Britain, France, Germany, Portugal, Belgium and Spain. The systematic exploitation of Africa by the European imperialists at the beginning of this century was possible after the Berlin Conference in 1884–85 which divided Africa into Europe's 'spheres of influence'. The Berlin Conference temporarily stopped the European colonizers from fighting each other for the spoils of Africa. After Western Europe's partitioning of Africa, Britain consolidated its empire in Africa (Porter, 1984).

2 Strategies Adopted by Britain for the Colonization of Africa

According to the National Curriculum, the core unit of the fourth key stage is supposed to focus on twentieth-century history. It is therefore being suggested here that this topic examines the twentieth-century British colonization of Africa.

Britain adopted two types of colonies in Africa, the settler and non-settler colonies. Various coercive and subtle methods were used by the British to exploit the rich land of its African colonies and the labour of the Africans; this topic could examine some of these strategies (Rodney, 1972).

Many historians categorize all colonized people into one homogeneous group, but imperial nations, Britain among them, adopted different strategies for colonizing women, men and children. The few avenues that women had for economic independence through farming, for example, were taken away from them as bigger, more profitable (for the British) systems of farming were imposed upon them. A substantial majority of men in the colonies were forced into the migrant labour system whereby they had to work for a great part of the year away from their homes. Through the imposed poverty of their parents, children also suffered various hardships. Most had no access to education, and the few that did, received a particular form of education which prepared them to administer the colonial system without challenging it (Boserup, 1970).

An important element of the history of British colonialism is the resistance that the colonized women, men and young people mounted against their oppressor (Rodney, 1972). Often an impression is created to history students that the colonized gave up their land without a struggle because they were not sufficiently organized. Teachers may therefore wish to give their students information about the massive resistance that the colonized responded with, as well as the violence that the colonizers used to curb these challenges.

The aim of this topic is therefore to explore the different types of col-onies that Britain constructed in Africa, the numerous strategies that Britain adopted to colonize women, men and children and the resistance of the Africans against British rule.

3 The Development of Britain Through its Colonies

What was the British Empire's contribution to Britain? The development of Britain is related to the under-development of its colonies, not simply to the agricultural and industrial revolutions and the 'trading' links that it had with countries overseas. Without the resources from Britain's colonies, Britain's industrial revolution would never have taken off. The slave plantations and the cash crop farms produced much more profit for Britain than the revolu-tionary forms of farming in Britain ever did (Rodney, 1972). For these reasons, the dialectical nature of Britain's development cannot be avoided, however much this government would like history teachers to do just that. For centuries the British state has nurtured an inaccurate image about Britain's develop-ment. In a small way, this topic could redress the imbalance.

An examination of the numerous ways in which Britain benefited from its glorious empire is interesting. The wealth that Britain extracted from its colonies contributed towards making it 'Great'. This wealth helped Britain build its capital, infrastructure, industry, and its welfare state, with its education, health and social services for all. Although the people of Britain gained at the expense of the people in its empire, women and men from different classes gained unevenly (Worsley, 1984).

4 The Consequences for the African Colonies under British Rule

Colonialism was devastating for all groups of people in the colonies. How-ever, women and men experienced colonialism in different ways, as did the upper and the subordinate classes. A study of these differences is vital for the understanding of the complex and dynamic force of colonialism (Nkrumah, 1963). The legacy of British imperialism for the colonies continues today (Sivanandan, 1989). This topic could also dispel the myth that various coun-tries in Africa and Asia are poor because its people are 'backward' as the historical consequences of colonialism are examined in detail.

For the fourth key stage, the National History Curriculum recommends that:

Pupils should be introduced to the causes, nature and consequences of conflict and co-operation between nations, with particular refer-ence to the Second World War and its impact. (DES, 1991, p. 51)

There are numerous explanations for the cause of the Second 'World War' and teachers may wish to encourage students to explore the European and the Third World perspectives. People in the Third World often refer to the First and the Second World Wars as the creation of the Europeans. This is because they consider that this tragedy was the result of conflict within the western European nations. In Europe, the disaster of the First World War had given rise to fascism in Italy, and the disaster of the 1920s depression had given rise to nazism in Germany. These two forms of dictatorships worked towards achieving economic dominance by a ruthless force. These European crises resulted in a war which dragged thousands of people of this world to their death (Porter, 1984).

5 Britain's Post-war Role in the Creation of the State of Israel

Britain played a special role in the colonization of Palestine. Not many people see Israel as a settler colony occupied by a group of Europeans. A detailed study of the creation of the state of Israel is interesting, because it illustrates that, beyond the impression created by the mass media, numerous powerful forces contributed towards the building of this colony. Students could explore the role that Britain played in the creation of the state of Israel. In studying the colonization of Palestine, two significant issues are: the manner in which the Palestinians have been displaced in their own country and the position of the Palestinians in Israel today (Frangi, 1982).

6 Anti-colonial Struggles in Africa and India

The National Curriculum expects students to be taught about the 'reasons for the break-up of the overseas empires of the European countries' (DES, 1991, p. 51). Here is an excellent opportunity to explore with the students the colonized people's long history of struggles for justice. Anti-colonial struggles began on the day the imperialists began their colonial mission (Porter, 1984). The study of anti-colonial struggles could challenge several myths. British imperial history is not a history of the civilizing of backward peoples, it is a history of violence and oppression. The colonized were never a group of docile people who were grateful to the British and other Europeans for governing their countries for them.

7 The Legacy of Colonialism

The colonial system drained the colonies of the wealth produced by the colonized peoples' labour, land and natural resources. This expropriation of resources did not stop with the independence of the colonies. It has continued.

The independent countries have had to join a world of trade and exchange that has been organized by the richer countries for centuries. Once the colonial powers surrendered their colonies, they did not change their unequal trading relationships with the poorer countries. Thus the wealth-transfer continues (Sivanandan, 1989). Teachers could assert that an examination of the ongoing processes which contribute toward some countries becoming developed and other countries remaining underdeveloped is in line with the National Curriculum's recommendation that 'pupils should be taught to understand how the world in which they live has been shaped by developments in twentieth-century history' (DES, 1991, p. 49).

The topics listed above would not meet all the requirements of the National Curriculum for Key Stage Four. Other topics specifically stipulated by the National Curriculum would also need to be included, for example: the extension of the parliamentary franchise in Britain, the reasons for change in the political party system, the differences between British democracy and other political systems, the relations between different parts of the United Kingdom and between the United Kingdom and the Irish Free State, etc. Since sixteen-year-old students who do the full history course will be examined by a national examination, it is important to ensure that they are taught all the areas of history stipulated by the National Curriculum. The topics suggested here could be interwoven into the teaching programme as and when the opportunity arises within the boundaries imposed by the National Curriculum.

The full history course for fourteen- to sixteen-year-old students consists of the core unit discussed above and the following two supplementary study units:

1   A thematic unit designed to deepen pupil's understanding of chronology and built on historical studies in earlier key stages. The National Curriculum expects this unit to:

    — be drawn from British history;
    — involve study over a long time span (starting at least 1500 AD and continuing to the present day);
    — give explicit attention to chronology;
      compare developments in different periods;
    — be based on a key historical theme, for example: Parliament, Public Health, Education, Agriculture, Work, Migration, Popular culture.

2   A unit involving a detailed study of the twentieth-century history of a country or region of the world other than Britain, chosen from:

    — Russia and the USSR, 1905 to 1964 (from the 1905 Revolution to the fall of Khrushchev);

— The United States of America, 1917 to 1963 (from the entry
of the USA into the First World War to the assassination of
President Kennedy);
— The Indian sub-continent, 1914 to 1964 (from the First World
War to the death of Nehru);
— Africa south of the Sahara, 1890 to 1963 (from the Boer
War to the independence of Kenya);
— The Middle East, 1914 to 1967 (from the First World War
to the Six Day Arab-Israeli War);
— Latin America, 1910 to 1962 (from the Mexican Revolution
to the Cuban Crisis);
— China, 1911 to 1966 (from the Chinese Revolution to the
'Cultural Revolution'). (DES, 1991, pp. 53–54)

The choice and flexibility offered to teachers through these two supplementary units is good. The units offer a useful opportunity for structuring lessons
using a people-centred historical perspective. Such opportunities must be
seized now for the young people in our society. When the British government
produces stricter guidelines for history teachers, other strategies for offering
students a people's history will have to be found. The supplementary units
for Key Stage Four could be developed in the same way as suggested for Key
Stage Two earlier.

The suggestions made in this chapter illustrate how gender, race and
class perspectives can be woven legitimately into the National Curriculum.
Following the National History Curriculum (England and Wales) uncritically
will result in the reinforcing of an Anglocentric view of history. The National
History Curriculum is the British government's effort to teach students a
limited history, a history that does not threaten the British social order with its
unequal class, race and gender relations. This limited history does not present
a balanced picture about the historic contribution of the people who built
Britain. The great contribution of the British working-class women, men and
children and the peoples of the British colonies is minimized or disregarded.
Through the denial of the exploitive role that Britain has played through
history, the British Conservative government hopes that the present day
oppressive social relations will remain unchallenged. History teachers can
either choose to flow with this historic British tide, thereby colluding with
repressive forces of this society, or they may choose to pave new roads and
offer their students some insight into the forces of oppression and liberation.

Chapter 5

Weaving a People's History into the National Curriculum

The National History Curriculum (England and Wales) does not make it obligatory for teachers to follow detailed lesson plans produced by the state. The curriculum, though prescriptive in many ways, still offers teachers opportunities for choosing their own teaching materials. Some overworked teachers may choose to minimize the amount of their work and follow the National Curriculum (DES, 1991) and the Non-Statutory Guidance of the National Curriculum Council (NCC, 1991) without making major additions or changes. Other teachers may wish to take the opportunities that the National Curriculum offers for creative planning of history lessons and organize the teaching in such a way that they encourage students to develop a critical analysis of historical development.

This chapter offers outlines for lesson plans which teachers can elaborate on according to the needs of their students. The aim of these lesson plan outlines is to illustrate how an anti-racist thread can be woven into history lessons despite the boundaries imposed by the National Curriculum. These brief lesson plans are designed to meet the requirements of the Attainment Targets outlined by the National History Curriculum (DES, 1991, pp. 3–10). The attainment targets and their constituent statements of attainment that follow the lesson plans specify the knowledge, skills and understanding which students are expected to have by the end of the programmes of study outlined below. These statements of attainment targets have been developed according to the format outlined by the National History Curriculum (England).

The following lesson plan outlines are for Key Stage Two, (eight to eleven year old students) Key Stage Three, (twelve to fourteen year old students) and Key Stage Four, (fifteen and sixteen year old students). The chapter does not include specific lesson plans for the first key stage which is intended for five to seven year old students because for this particular age group, the teaching of history would focus very much on the history of the students' own families and communities. When it is appropriate for teachers to include the history of other groups of people and countries for this age group, teachers may wish to adapt some of the lesson plan outlines in this chapter. The material from the lesson plans on the ancient civilizations of Egypt and India, for example, could effectively be used for teaching the history of people who lived a very long time ago to seven year old students. Similarly, the lesson plan outline on the resistance of the slaves could be elaborated to teach about black heroines from the past.

These study areas have been designed with an assumption that history teaching should encourage students to develop historical skills within the context of investigating the history of how people lived in the past and related to each other. The aim is, therefore, to offer students an opportunity to develop historical skills of evaluation, abstraction, analysis, synthesis, empathy and communication while exploring the social, economic and political relationships between groups of people through history. Students would learn about the courts of the Tudor and Stuart monarchs (Section one of Key Stage 2) and about the architecture of medieval times (Section four of Key Stage 3) and learn in detail about the slave trade during the Tudor and the Stuart times (Section four 'The Beginnings of the British Empire' of KS2) and the medieval colonization of Ireland (Supplementary Unit A of KS3). Some of the other areas of study that the lesson plans cover include: The Ancient Civilizations of Egypt and the Indus Valley, Britain's development through colonization, the role of education in Britain's former colonies, the development of racism as an ideology, the oppression of first-nation people of North America, anti-colonial struggles in India and the founding of the state of Israel. A lesson plan on Ireland has also been included to illustrate that it was in Ireland that Britain perfected the art of conquest and domination prior to the expansion into the countries further away.

In the process of exploring the past, it is hoped that students will learn to locate information from a range of sources, recognize bias, omissions and irrelevancies, situate the evidence within a historical context and communicate their findings in a variety of imaginative reconstructions, such as plays, exhibitions, projects, etc. Most important, it is hoped that students will gain some understanding of the dialectical nature of history, that history is not a study of isolated, unrelated incidents of the past, but it is a critical exploration of the historical social, economic and political forces that have had an impact upon groups of people in the past and continue to do so today. These lesson plans have been chosen to illustrate that, with creative planning and determination, teachers can still offer their students some insights into the forces of oppression and resistance through history, thus liberating the National History Curriculum.

Key Stage Two: Core Study Unit Two

Key Stage Two has a small section in Core Study Unit 'Tudor and Stuart times' entitled 'The beginnings of the British Empire'. This significant part of

British history is included in a section with 'explorers, including Drake and Raleigh, and their voyages'. This core study unit also includes topics such as the court life of the Tudor and Stuart rulers, events such as the break with Rome, the Armada, the Gunpowder Plot, the Civil War, the Restoration, the Great Plague, the Great Fire of London, etc.

The section on the beginning of the British Empire is only a small part of this core study unit. Nevertheless, such opportunities need to be utilized in order to offer students a broad and balanced history. The following study plan is offered as a suggestion. The aim of this study plan is to ensure that students gain sufficient information about the beginning of the British Empire so that they can understand:

1 the aim of British colonialism;
2 the strategies adopted by Britain for building its empire;
3 the development of Britain through its colonies;
4 the underdevelopment of the British colonies through their experience of British colonialism.

Students' Work Sheet

The Beginnings of the British Empire

Exercise 1: The Colonization of the Caribbean Islands

The first British contact with the Caribbean was in the middle of the sixteenth century. The first crop that the British successfully grew in the Caribbean was tobacco. The early settlers employed British paupers and prisoners as labourers. When sugar was found to be a more profitable crop, the small tobacco farms were changed into large sugar cane plantations. The cultivation of sugar required much more work than the tobacco production did. The British planters turned to West Africa for the extra labour force needed on the new plantations. This is when Britain began to buy and sell African people to grow sugar cane in the Caribbean. This trade in people was carried out between 1562 and 1807 by the British and many other European countries. Millions of African people were enslaved or died as a result of activities related to slavery, such as captivity after being kidnapped, the journey to the African coast or the journey by sea to the Caribbean. Even when the African people made it to the Caribbean, the harsh work and conditions of living resulted in many premature deaths.

Question: How did Britain extract the wealth of the Caribbean Islands from the sixteenth to the nineteenth century?

Exercise 2: The Triangular Trade

We were dispersed throughout the Americas, the fruits of our labour were all ploughed back into Europe together with the huge profits resulting from the sale of endless shiploads of slaves. The cotton and the sugar we produced provided employment in Europe's developing manufacturing and refining industries, whose surplus products were, in turn, shipped back to Africa to begin the whole cycle again. The overall benefits from this triangular venture were enormous and eventually turned Britain and France into the strongest trading nations in the world. Most important of all, however, is the fact that it was the blood, sweat and tears of black women and men which financed and serviced Europe's Industrial Revolution, a revolution which laid the basis for Europe's subsequent domination and monopoly of the world's resources. (Bryan, *et al.*, 1985, p. 6)

Question: How did Britain benefit from the slave trade?

Exercise 3: Justifications for Slavery and Colonialism

The buying and the selling of human beings for the purpose of making them work without paying them any wages was justified by the Europeans in many ways. As slavery became a highly profitable activity, the slavers began to believe that African people were inferior to the Europeans and therefore it did not matter how Africans were treated:

I am apt to believe that the Negroes and in general all the other species of men (for there are four or five different kinds) to be naturally inferior to the Whites. There scarcely ever was a civilized nation of that complexion, not any individual, eminent either in action or speculation. (David Hume, 1748, quoted by Fryer, 1984, p. 152)

Some British scientists tried to argue that African people were closer to monkeys than to human beings:

The Negro structure approximates unequivocally to that of the monkey . . . I deem the moral and intellectual character of the Negro inferior, and decidedly so, to that of the European. (Sir William Lawrence, 1819, quoted by Fryer, 1984, p. 170)

Some British Christians argued that God had wanted African people to be the servants of white people. Africans were seen as:

... the only Savage of all the coloured races that doesn't die out of sight of the White Man; but can actually live besides him, and work and increase and be merry. The Almighty Maker has appointed him to be a Servant. (Carlyle, 1867, quoted by Fryer, 1984, p. 172)

Many British people therefore began to believe that Africans were inferior to Europeans, closer to animals, and God-sent servants. British people also started to believe that they were the greatest people in the world and therefore should rule the world:

I believe that the British race is the greatest of governing races the world has ever seen. (Cheers). I say this not merely as an empty boast, but as proved and shown by the success which we have had in administering vast dominions. (Colonial Secretary Joseph Chamberlain, 1895, quoted by Fryer, P., 1984, p. 183)

By the end of the nineteenth century literary artists, such as Kipling reinforced these ideas:

Take up the white man's burden,
Send forth the best ye breed,
Go bind your sons to exile,
To serve your captive's need:
To wait in heavy harness,
On fluttered fold and wild,
Your new caught, sullen people,
Half devil and half child.
(from Kipling, R. (1977) *Selected Verses*, Harmondsworth,
Penguin, p. 326)

Such racist ideas and theories did not take into account the fact that before the European's slave system was established in Africa, the people of Africa lived in various forms of communities: small self-sufficient agricultural and hunting groups, village communities with intricate social and economic structures, large towns with complex political systems and large city states with sophisticated forms of government. Furthermore, the people of Africa have a long history of creativity. The Egyptian civilization of 5000 years ago for example, had a complex form of government, extraordinary buildings such as the pyramids, temples and palaces, systems of recording and writing, numerous forms of art and various expressions of religious and philosophical thought.

Question: Do ideas about black people being inferior and white people being superior still exist in Britain today? Give examples.

Exercise 4: The Colonization of India

In the seventeenth century, British traders went to India to buy exotic cloth: muslin, velvet, silk, and fine cotton. With the wealth created by the slave trade, Britain was able to build huge machines for the mass production of cotton. However, the British weather was not suitable for growing cotton, and raw cotton had to be imported into Britain from overseas. One of Britain's sources of raw cotton was its Caribbean plantations. Britain's other major source of raw cotton was its Indian colony.

In order to export raw cotton from India, Britain made it difficult for Indian cotton manufacturers to export their finished product to Britain by imposing heavy taxes on the Indian merchants. Many Indian cotton factories had to be closed and Indian farmers were forced to sell their raw cotton to British merchants. Once the cotton had been woven in the British mills, the British merchants sold their cotton goods to the people of Britain, India and many other countries. In this way, many people in Britain gained employment in the mills, the British merchants became rich, and poverty struck the Indian mill workers, merchants and their families.

Question: After Britain colonized India, British cotton mills began to flourish and the Indian cotton industry collapsed. Explain how this came about.

Exercise 5: One of the Aims of the British Empire

I was employed in the East End of London yesterday and attended a meeting of the unemployed. I listened to the wild speeches which were just a cry of 'bread! bread!' and on my way home I pondered over the scene and I became more convinced of the importance of imperialism ... My cherished idea is a solution for the social problem, i.e., in order to save the 40,000,000 inhabitants of the United Kingdom from a bloody civil war, we colonial statesmen must acquire new lands to settle the surplus population, to provide new markets for the goods produced in the factories and mines. The Empire, as I have always said, is a bread and butter question. If you want to avoid a civil war, you just become imperialists. (Cecil Rhodes, 1895, in Institute of Race Relations, 1982, *Patterns of Racism*, London, p. 21)

Question: What were the benefits of colonialism for Britain according to the writer above?

Exercise 6: Britain's Sources of Raw Materials

The colonies, such as the West Indies, India, West Africa and Malaya were a source of raw material for Britain. Some of the raw materials were sugar, tea, cocoa beans, oil palm nuts, rubber, jute and cotton. Numerous manufacturing industries in London, York, Dundee, Lancashire, Birmingham, Liverpool and the Midlands benefited from these raw materials. The finished produce from the factories in Britain were then sold to the people in Britain, Europe and in the British colonies.

Written Work

Write an essay on how Britain gained from its empire and how the colonies lost their resources.

Discussion

Some people believe that Britain's technical inventions made a major contribution towards the industrial revolution. Discuss the contribution of the slave trade, the slave plantations and the colonies of the British Empire to Britain's industrial revolution.

Teacher's Resource List

BRYAN, B., DADZIE, S. and SCAFE, S. (1985) *The Heart of the Race*, London, Virago.

FRYER, P. (1984) *Staying Power: The History of Black People in Britain*, London, Pluto Press.

FRYER, P. (1988) *Black People in the British Empire: An Introduction*, London, Pluto Press.

SANDWELL DEPARTMENT OF EDUCATION (1987) *Britain and India: An Uncommon Journey*, (Units 1, 2 & 3) Sandwell, Education Development Centre.

Key Stage Two: Core Study Unit Four

Key Stage Two 'Britain since 1930', has a section 'immigration and emigration'. Although this unit deals primarily with Britain since 1930, to really comprehend the process of Britain's migration patterns, it is necessary, to explore the history of the British peoples' emigration to the countries of the British Empire and the post-war immigration of black people into Britain. The aim of this lesson plan is to encourage students to examine some of the factors that have affected Britain's immigration and emigration patterns.

Students' Work Sheet

Britain's Colonial Emigration and Post-colonial Immigration

For several centuries, British people have gone to live in many countries of this world. Some of these countries were the countries of black people for example India, South Africa, Aden, Australia, etc. Why did British people go to live in these countries? Black people have also immigrated to Britain especially after the Second World War. Why have black people come to live in Britain? To understand some of these question fully, we need to examine the historical relationship that Britain has had with many countries of black people. Britain had one of the biggest empires in the world. During the colonial era, many British people went to live and work in the countries of their empire. The British people who emigrated to the colonies went to serve their empire and in doing so, they helped to achieve the aims of their empire.

The fundamental aim of the British Empire was to make profit. This it did in numerous ways, for example, by using the colonies as cheap sources of raw material. Often the people of the British colonies were forced to work for very low wages to produce raw materials such as sugar cane, cotton and ground nuts for Britain. These raw materials were shipped to Britain and manufactured into finished products. In doing this, the manufacturing industries of Britain flourished and the colonies were stopped from developing their own industries. Britain made further profits by selling the finished products, sugar, cloth and oil, to the people of its colonies at high prices. This process created employment, industrial development and wealth in Britain and unemployment, underdevelopment and poverty in the colonies.

In some of the British colonies, for example in Kenya, the British emigrants took the richest land away from the local farmers and settled on this land themselves. The British government made such changes in the ownership of land possible through the laws that it passed as the ruler of Kenya. Therefore, while the people of Kenya who were evicted from their land suffered from landlessness and poverty, the British emigrants were able to live in luxury.

The British emigrants who went to live in the countries of their empire administered many systems for the benefit of their own country — Great Britain. One example is the tax system that was instituted in Britain's colonies. In many African colonies, the African people had to pay taxes to the British for living in their own huts, for fishing in their own African lakes, for hunting in their forests, etc. These taxes were not used for providing services to the African communities but were used by the British to administer the systems which made their rule possible.

The people of the British Empire resisted against their colonizers and most colonies eventually achieved independence. However, through the three centuries of colonialism, Britain became rich and developed and the people of the colonies suffered landlessness, unemployment and poverty.

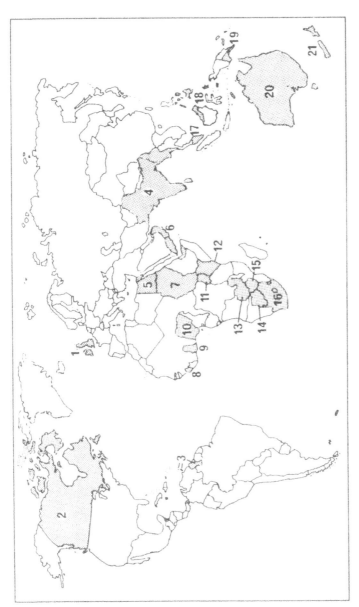

This is a map of the British Empire. The shaded areas show British "Possessions" in 1914 *some* of the countries of the British Empire are numbered on the map. Can you find out the names of these countries?

Figure 1: The British Empire in 1914

The countries that have been systematically underdeveloped for decades and in some cases for centuries continue to lag behind the countries that have achieved development by using the resources of huge parts of this world. For these reasons, some people have emigrated from under-developed countries with hopes of a decent life and employment. The descendants of the unemployed and the landless people of the colonies of the British Empire have come to live in Britain. Many black people also came to Britain after the Second World War because the British Government invited them to come and help to rebuild the war torn country.

The majority of the people who have immigrated to Britain have come from the countries that the people of Britain once colonized. Not all people who have come to work and live in Britain are black. White people from Europe, Australia, New Zealand, Canada, the United States, etc. have also settled in Britain. Furthermore, not all black people are immigrants, for many black people have lived in Britain for generations and see themselves as British.

Project

Africa was colonized by many different European countries (see map page 83). Choose two countries of Africa and find out about how these countries experienced colonialism.

Discussion

Why did the British people go to live in the countries of their Empire?
Why have black people come to live in Britain?
Are all immigrants in Britain black?

Resource Books for Teachers

INSTITUTE OF RACE RELATIONS (1982) Book One, *Roots of Racism*, London, Institute of Race Relations.
INSTITUTE OF RACE RELATIONS (1982) Book Two, *Patterns of Racism*, London, Institute of Race Relations.
INSTITUTE OF RACE RELATIONS (1985) Book Three, *How Racism came to Britain*, London, Institute of Race Relations.
SANDWELL DEPARTMENT OF EDUCATION (1987) *Britain and India: An Uncommon Journey*, (Units 1, 2 & 3) Sandwell, Education Development Centre.
SIVANANDAN, A. (1982) *A Different Hunger: Writings on Black Resistance*, London, Pluto Press.

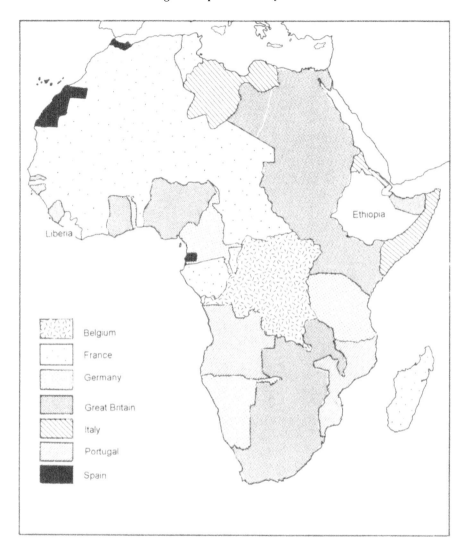

Figure 2: The colonial partition of Africa in 1914.

Key Stage Two: Core Study Unit Five

Study Unit One

Key Stage Two: Core Study Unit Five is about Ancient Greece. This study unit does not acknowledge the contribution of black civilisations to the development of Ancient Greece. By ignoring the dynamic relationship that existed between the people of Africa, Asia and Greece during the flowering of the Greek culture, Eurocentric notions about the Greek civilization are reinforced. The following lesson plan aims to examine the process by which the contribution of black civilisations to this world has been masked over the years. Through this examination, it is hoped that students will appreciate the inter-relationships and the contribution of all ancient civilizations to this world.

Students' Work Sheet

The Denial of the Contribution of the Black Civilizations to this World

Palaeontological evidence suggests that the first human beings lived on the continent of Africa. Gradually, people from Africa moved to Europe and to Asia. By adapting to the different environments, early human beings began to develop their own regional characteristics and identities. As time went by, the early human beings developed ways of surviving in groups by hunting together during the day and by offering each other protection against the wild animals at night. Gradually, they learned to grow food and domesticate animals and to live in larger groups.

By 3000 BC human beings had begun to live in complex social organizations — the ancient civilizations. The following map illustrates the geographical area covered by the ancient civilizations. The oldest civilization existed in Egypt, Africa, 3000BC. The West Asian civilizations which existed between 2800BC and AD500 included Sumer, Akkad, Babylonia, Assyria, Mitanni, Syria, Israel Troy and Persia. The Indian civilizations of the period between 2700BC and AD300 included the Indus Valley civilization and the empires of the Mauryas and the Guptas. The civilizations which existed in Europe between 2000BC and AD400 included the civilizations of the Minoans, Mycenaeans, Greeks and the Romans. The Roman Empire covered much of the south of Europe and parts of Britain.

The African and Asian civilizations had complex systems of government, extraordinary temples and palaces, systems of recording and writing, beautiful examples of art and various expressions of religious worship and philosophical thought. The civilizations of Africa and Asia existed before the European civilizations. Nevertheless some historians and scholars such as Lord Delcare argue that only Europe has ever witnessed human development and advancement.

Perhaps, in the future, there will be some African history to teach. But at present there is none, or very little: there is only the history of the Europeans in Africa. The rest is largely darkness, like the history of pre-European, pre-Columbian America. And darkness is not a subject for history.

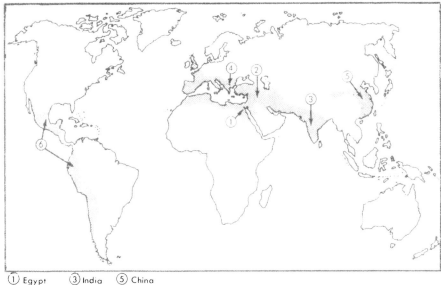

① Egypt   ③ India   ⑤ China
② West Asia   ④ Europe   ⑥ America

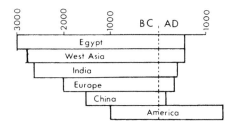

Figure 3: Ancient civilizations of the world.

It is European techniques, European examples, European ideas, which have shaken the non-European world out of its past — out of barbarism in Africa, out of a far older, slower, more majestic civilization in Asia; and the history of the world, for the last five centuries, in so far as it has significance, has been European history (Hugh Trevor-Roper, now Lord Declare, 1966, in Chirimuuta and Chirimuuta, 1987 Asia, Africa and Racism, Bretby, Chirimuuta).

However, civilizations were thriving in Africa and Asia long before the European civilizations existed. As the movement of people continued from

Africa to other parts of the world, so they carried with them some of the ideas and techniques from the oldest civilization of Egypt to other parts of the world. Some historians, for example Willetts, are able to acknowledge this process. Willetts writes about how the first civilization that evolved in Europe around 2000BC was influenced by the older African and Asian civilizations.

> The Minoans created the first major Aegean civilization comparable in its enduring achievements with the older civilizations of the ancient world in Egypt, Mesopotamia and Anatolia. In the process they demonstrated how a small area of the earth's surface inhabited by inventive people, bounded by the sea and immune from aggressive conquerors for many centuries, could be receptive to, but not dominated by, influences flowing from the vast continents of Asia and Africa. (Willetts in Cotterell, 1987, p. 204)

The ancient civilization of Greece dates back to around 700BC and indeed Greece had many links with Africa and Asia. Many scholars from Greece went to study in Egypt. Also, Greece had numerous trading links with the countries of Africa and Asia. Through these trading links, people of Africa, Asia and Europe exchanged not only goods but ideas too. This was another way in which people from different cultures learned from each other.

In 327 BC the Greek emperor Alexander went to conquer northern India but did not succeed. On his journeys, Alexander had with him a number of Greeks who recorded their impressions of the people that they met. Of the Indian people that Alexander and his men came across, one of the scribes wrote:

> The dress worn by the Indians is made of cotton produced on trees ... They wear an undergarment of cotton which reaches below the knee halfway down to the ankles and an upper garment which they throw partly over their shoulders and partly twist in folds round their head. The Indians also wear earrings of ivory, but only the very wealthy do this. They use parasols as a screen from the heat. They wear shoes made of white leather and these are elaborately trimmed, while the soles are variegated, and made of great thickness, to make the wearer seem so much taller. (Thapar, R. (1966) A History of Indian, London, Penguin, p. 60)

The Greek scribes also wrote about how the Indian people governed themselves, worshipped, produced agricultural produce etc ... The records of Alexander's scribes are another example of how ideas travelled from one continent to another more than two thousand years ago.

We have seen that the people of Africa, Asia and Europe had various links with each other and through such contact, learned from each other. Prior to the emergence of ancient Greece, Europe had witnessed the rise and fall of the Minoan and the Mycenaean civilizations. The Minoan and the

Mycenaean people were influenced by the cultures of black people for they had links with the people of the older civilizations of Africa and Asia. Similarly, the people of ancient Greece were also influenced by the cultures of black people.

The following extract from the National History Curriculum (England) shows the areas that the British Government expects students to learn about the Greek civilization.

Key Stage Two: Core Study Unit Five

Ancient Greece

Pupils should be introduced to the civilization of ancient Greece and its legacy to the modern world. The focus should be on the way of life, beliefs and achievements of the ancient Greeks.

Pupils should be taught about:

the city state: Athens and Sparta, citizens and slaves;
the economy: agriculture and trade sea transport;
everyday life: the lives of men, women and children, sport;
Greek religion and thought: Greek gods and religious practices, myths and legends, scientists and philosophers;
the arts: architecture, art, drama and literature, and how they reflected Greek society;
relations with other peoples: the Persian Wars, Greece and Rome (DES, 1991, History in the National Curriculum (England), HMSO, p. 27)

This National Curriculum study plan does not offer many opportunities to learn about the links that ancient Greece had with Africa and Asia. By not acknowledging and studying the contribution of the African and Asian civilization to Ancient Greece, an impression could easily be created that the Greeks were the creators of civilization. When scholars such as Lord Declare quoted above argue that world civilization is rooted in Europe and that the black people of Africa and Asia never had the intelligence and scientific knowledge to build and organize complex societies, to express philosophical thought or to produce sophisticated forms of art a Eurocentric view of history is created. Why do you think that the National History Curriculum of Britain does not include the study of the contribution of black people to the civilization of ancient Greece?

Project Work

Question: African and Asian civilizations have made a major contribution to the civilizations of Greece and Rome, and yet this contribution is not always acknowledged. Why do you think this is so?

Resource Books for Teachers

BERNAL, M. (1987) *Black Athena: The Afroasiatic Roots of Classical Civilization*, (Volume 1) London, Free Association Books.
COTTERELL, A. (1980) *The Penguin Encyclopedia of Ancient Civilizations*, London, Penguin.

Key Stage Two: Supplementary Unit C

This Supplementary Unit includes a study of a past non-European society, Ancient Egypt, Mesopotamia, Assyria, The Indus Valley, The Maya or Benin. The following study plan is suggested as part of the study of Ancient Egypt. The aim is to encourage students to examine the Egyptian civilization from a variety of perspectives: political, social, economic and scientific.

Students' Work Sheet

The Ancient Civilizations of Egypt

The River Nile in Africa occupies a very special place in history, for it was along its banks that the great civilization of Egypt grew five thousand years ago.

*The Egyptian People's Understanding of their Environment
Five Thousand Years Ago*

Surrounded by the desert, the peoples of the ancient civilization of Egypt lived along the fertile banks of the River Nile. They had to learn to understand the river and to control its flooding. They had to use the flood water for agricultural purposes, and at the same time, had to prevent damage to their settlements. The peoples of Egypt built dykes and dam walls to stop the water from flooding their villages, they built canals to help the water run through their fields. To do all of this, they needed a system of accurate measurement, so they developed early forms of mathematics and geometry.

The Ancient Egyptian People's Understanding of the Seasons

The calendar that we use today was also devised by the peoples of the Nile Valley. They found that the rhythm of life was marked by agricultural seasons: there was a time each year when the river flooded the land; when the land dried, it was time for planting; and this was followed by the harvest season. Then the river flooded again and the cycle recommenced. Days were counted by the phases of the moon, called months. The flood cycle began every 365 days and this 'year' was divided into twelve months or moon phases.

Egyptian Forms of Writing Five Thousand Years Ago

The Egyptians developed one of the first forms of writing, and they were the first to use it on a wide scale. The people who could write (scribes) noted the level of the flooding, the height of the dam walls, the depth and the distance of the irrigation ditches, the amount of grain stored at harvest time, and so on.

The Political Organization of the Egyptian Civilization

The civilization of Egypt was headed by the pharaoh. The pharaohs' governments were led by senior advisers, provincial rulers, army generals and priests. The means of production and the distribution of wealth was controlled by the state. Most of the people were farmers who lived and worked on the land which belonged to the pharaoh. Some people worked in the mines or the quarries. Other groups of workers included various craftspeople: bakers, potters, flower-arrangers, sculptors, goldsmiths, water-carriers, watchmen, dogkeepers, shepherds, goatherds, goose-herds. The craftspeople formed guilds to protect their skills and sometimes were organized enough to withdraw their services and go on strike if their payment or rations were delayed.

The Production and Distribution of Food in Ancient Egypt

The efficient growth and distribution of food was important for the survival of the Nile societies. Peasant farmers grew wheat and barley. The development of huge granaries made it possible for food supplies to last from year to year. The efficient river transport made it possible for food supplies to be shipped from one area to another. Because of the highly organized farming and the fertile soil, yields were generally very good. The surplus fed large numbers of government officials, workers in the ship yards, weapons factories, spinning mills, etc.

The Religion of the People of the Egyptian Civilization

The ancient Egyptians believed that heaven and earth were filled with spirits which lived in people, animals and in plants. They saw God's forces in the sun, the moon, the stars, the sky and the Nile floods. They also believed that

Figure 4: A drawing of wall paintings illustrating the life of people in the ancient civilization of Egypt. Note the various agricultural activities, particularly that of the surveying party whose job it was to measure plots of land, to estimate crop yields and to calculate the taxes payable.

the same rights and practices that governed life continued after death. Egyptian religion, art and ethics stressed the good of all the people rather than the individual. The law nevertheless was for the protection of the individual. Women and men had equal rights to justice.

Group Work

Do an exhibition of the Egyptian civilization. Illustrate the Egyptian people's method of producing and distributing food and highlight the Egyptian people's awareness of their environment.

Resource Books for Teachers

COTTERELL, A. (1980) *The Penguin Encyclopedia of Ancient Civilizations*, London, Penguin.
SIBANDA, M., MOYANA, H. and GUMBO, S.D. (1982) *The African Heritage*, Harare, Zimbabwe Educational Books.

BERNAL, M. (1987) *Black Athena: The Afroasiatic Roots of Classical Civilization*, (Volume 1), London, Free Association Books.

Key Stage Two: Supplementary Unit B

This unit allows students to learn about non-European societies. The following lesson plan explores the ancient Indus Valley civilization.

Students' Work Sheet

The Ancient Civilization of the Indus Valley

The discovery of the Indus Valley civilization in 1922 is one of the triumphs of modern archaeology. The story of this civilization is still fragmentary, but a great deal can be deducted from the 4500 year old remains that have been unearthed. The Indus Valley civilization covered an enormous geographical landscape, a gigantic triangle of a thousand miles long (see map, p. 92). This civilization consisted of big cities of which the two capitals Mohenjo-daro and Harappa were the biggest and numerous towns, villages and sea ports.

The City of Mohenjo-daro

From the archaeological finds, it is clear that there were many dwelling-houses of various sizes in the city of Mohenjo-daro. Some were small buildings with two rooms and others were palatial with walls that were four to five feet thick. They were made of good quality bricks which have survived thousands of years. The big houses had two or three storeys and were furnished with paved floors, courtyards, doors, windows and stairways. Every house was supplied by water from wells and had an intricate drainage system which enabled the waste water to be drained away in brick lined sewers. The houses also had rubbish-chutes which carried away other waste.

In addition to the dwelling houses, there were spacious buildings of elaborate structure and design. Some of these contained large pillared halls. These large buildings are thought to have been palaces, temples and municipal halls. In the cities and towns there were also numerous restaurants, shops and cafes.

The Great Bath of Mohenjo-daro

An interesting structure of the city is the Great Bath, with walls that were eight feet wide (see diagram on p. 93). This bath consisted of a large open

Figure 5: Ancient India: the Indus Valley covered a vast geographical area. Mohenjo-daro and Harappa were as far apart as London and Edinburgh.

quadrangle in the centre with galleries and rooms on all sides. In the centre of the quadrangle was a large swimming pool thirty-nine feet long, twenty-three feet wide and about eight feet deep. It had a flight of steps at either end and had a supply of water from a well situated in one of the adjoining rooms. The water was discharged by a huge drain.

City and Road Planning at Mohenjo-daro

The streets of the city were wide and straight and were also furnished with an elaborate drainage system. The layout of the houses and roads in the city indicate that a concerted effort had been made to plan the city rationally. The official and the residential areas were laid out on a regular grid pattern,

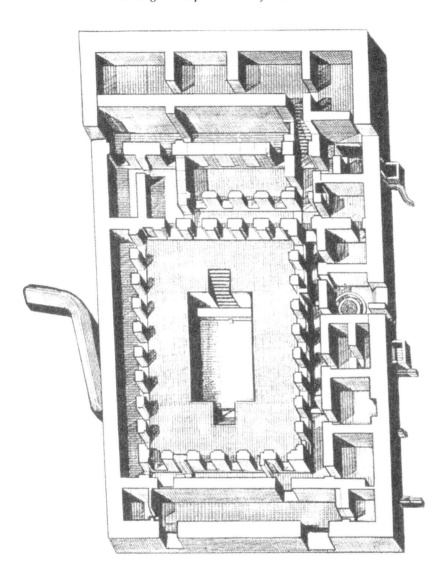

Figure 6. The Great Bath at Mohenjo daro.

with the main streets running north-south and smaller streets running into them east-west. There must have been a great flow of traffic along the main road, for sentry boxes have been excavated which were probably used for wardens to direct the traffic.

Question: Describe the organization of the ancient city of Mohenjo-daro and list the skills that must have been needed to build such a city.

The Government of the Indus Valley Civilization

Mohenjo-daro and Harappa, the two big cities of the Indus Valley civilization are about as far apart as London, England and Edinburgh, Scotland. Besides these two cities, there were also many other smaller towns and numerous villages scattered along the river and its tributaries. This vast stretch of towns and cities was probably overseen by one single government. Excavations of the area have shown that the bricks that were used for building houses and official buildings were made of the same size throughout the entire region of the Indus Valley civilization. Such uniformity suggests that the bricks were probably made according to one official specification. Weights and measures throughout the region were also standardized and this, too, suggests that systems of weighing and measuring were regulated by one central organization. For such a vast area to be governed by one body required a complex structure of organization and communication.

Activity: Try to imagine and write about how the government of the ancient Indus Valley managed to govern such a vast civilization.

The Economy of the Indus Valley

The Indus Valley civilization was dependant on agriculture. The people of the Indus Valley had to learn to understand their environment and control the flooding of the river Indus in order to maximize their agricultural production. With the aid of silt-bearing floods and irrigation the farmers cultivated many crops. This indicates that the Indus people had a good knowledge of the seasons and the ability to use mathematics and geometry for the purposes of irrigation.

The people of the Indus Valley cuitivated wheat, barley, vegetables, fruit, and sesame and mustard for oils. In the area of Lothal, rice cultivation had been mastered; this crop has been the staple dish for most of India ever since. Also, cotton was grown and manufactured throughout the Indus valley, and this process, too, required immense skill and craftsmanship. The people of the Indus Valley civilization had domesticated cats, dogs, camels, horses and elephants and reared sheep, humped and humpless cattle, buffalo and pigs.

Huge granaries have been excavated along the Indus Valley. These granaries were used for storing wheat, barley and rice. The farmers of the Indus Valley probably had to hand over part of their crops to the ruling authority, which more than likely took responsibility for its storage and distribution. It is possible that from this reserve of grain produce, public workers, such as surveyors, architects, builders, irrigation system developers, plumbers, traffic wardens, artists, musicians and others were paid for their services.

Craftspeople, such as weavers, knitters, potters, carpenters, masons, blacksmiths, goldsmiths, jewellers, ivory workers and toolmakers produced goods both for the home markets and foreign trade, which took place overland as well as across the oceans.

Activity: Describe the work of the agricultural workers, the public workers and the craftspeople of the Indus Valley civilization.

Trading Links of the People of the Civilization of the Indus Valley

The people of the ancient Indus Valley had extensive trading links with people of distant countries over land and across vast distances by sea. In Lothal, for example, there was a kiln-burned brick dockyard measuring 730×120 feet. Merchant ships entered at high tide through a specially designed channel. On the quay stood warehouses ready to discharge export items and store imported goods. From this port vessels sailed to places as far away as Bahrein in the Persian Gulf and the cities of Mesopotamia. Bahrein was Tilmun, the legendary Sumerian paradise. At Tilmun, the influence of the Indus merchants was strong as excavations have shown that the weights and measures used in the Indus Valley prevailed in this distant land too. This is an example of people exchanging ideas while trading.

Question: What skills did the people of the Indus valley need in order to trade with foreign countries?

Dress and Ornaments of the People of the Ancient Indus Valley

From the excavations, we can get some idea of the people of the Indus Valley civilization. They wore clothes made of cotton and wool. Ornaments were worn by women and men of all classes. Necklaces, fillets, armlets, finger-rings and bangles were worn by both women and men, and girdles, nose-studs, earrings and anklets were worn by women alone. There was a great variety in the shapes and design of these ornaments. These ornaments were made of gold, silver, ivory, copper and both precious and semi-precious stones like jade, crystal agate, carnelian and lapis lazuli.

Household Articles of the People of the Indus Valley Civilization

Household articles included earthenware vessels of a rich variety which were made with a potter's wheel and were either plain or painted; some were even glazed. Ornamental vessels of copper, bronze, silver and porcelain were also made. Other articles of domestic use included spindles and spindle whorls made of baked earth, porcelain and shell; needles and combs made of bone or ivory; axes, chisels, knives, sickles, fishhooks and razors made of copper and bronze and small cubical blocks of hard stone which were probably used as weights. Children's toys included, dolls, small wheeled carts and chairs and dice-pieces.

Question: For what were the household articles unearthed by archaeologists used by the people of the ancient Indus Valley?

Skills and Technical Knowledge of the People of the Civilization of the Indus Valley

A great advance in technical knowledge is indicated by the potters wheel, kiln-burnt brick, the boring of hard substances like carnelian, and the casting and alloy of metals. A high aesthetic sense is indicated by the beautiful designs of ornaments and the execution of fine stone statues.

Activity: Can you find out more about the skills of pottery, brick making, boring of hard substances and casting and alloy of metals?

Religion of the People of the Ancient Indus Valley

The objects found at the sites of the Indus Valley civilization also teach us something about the religious faiths and beliefs of the people of these ancient times. Many figurines of female and male gods have been unearthed. The widespread worshipping of the Divine Mother Goddess indicates that the people of the ancient Indus Valley believed in a female energy as the source of all creation.

The Writing of the People of the Indus Valley Civilization

The people of the Indus had a form of writing which present day hieroglyphic experts have not as yet been able to decipher. The writing of the Indus people has been left behind by them on thousands of soapstone seals. We hope that one day scholars will succeed in reading the writing left behind by this civilization, and we will have greater insights into the thoughts and lives of the peoples of the Indus Valley civilization.

Activity: Try to devise a system of writing with your own signs and symbols to keep account of trade and see if your friends can figure it out.

Project Work

Find out about the organization of the Mauryan Empire that existed in India between 321–185 BC.

Resource Books for Teachers

COTTERELL, A. (1980) *The Penguin Encyclopedia of Ancient Civilizations*, London, Penguin.

MAJUMDAR, R.C., DATTA, K. and RAYCHAUDHURI, H.C. (1946) *An Advanced History of India*, London, Macmillan.

Key Stage Three: Core Study Unit Two

This unit is titled 'Medieval realms: Britain 1066 to 1500' and includes a section 'Britain and the wider world — the idea of Christendom and the extent to which the British Isles were part of a wider European world'.

The idea of Christendom in the medieval period is most interesting. It was a period when tens of thousands of European Christian women, men and children went on horse and foot to conquer the lands of non-Christian peoples. The Crusades were significant in that they paved the way for the later European domination of the world. The aims of the lesson plan are to:

1 Explore the process which drove European Christians to conquer the lands of other people;
2 Examine the religious, economic, social and political aims of the Crusades and how these affected the people who had been conquered.

Students' Work Sheet 1

The Crusades of the European Christendom

During the period 1066 to 1500, the Christian Church was a dominant force within the European society. The Church regulated the society by guiding people's thinking, attitudes and beliefs. From this powerful position, in the eleventh century, under the organizing influence of the popes, the holy warriors of Christendom were sent to conquer the territory of people who were not Christians. This was possible because the Roman Catholic Church had divided all human beings into Christians and non-Christians. People who were not Christian were seen as 'heathens', 'infidels' and 'heretics' and, as a general rule, the Church made the lands and the peoples of the non-Christian world the property of the Crusaders. The Roman Catholic Church gradually attained

Figure 7: The Crusaders believed that to kill or to take into slavery a non-Christian was to serve the highest purpose of God.

religious, economic and ideological dominance. The first Crusades may be taken as the starting point of the process which finally led to the world domination by Europeans.

The guiding philosophy of the Christian church, during the period 1066 to 1500 was that to kill or to take into slavery a non-Christian (a heathen, infidel or heretic), was to serve the highest purpose of God. One historian, Azurara, writing in the middle of the fifteenth century, explained that people who enslaved non-Christians believed that although the 'bodies [of the slaves] were now brought into subjection, that was a small matter in comparison to their soul, which would now possess true freedom for evermore' (Cox, 1970, p. 328).

Project Work

Outline the religious, aims of the Crusades and how these affected the people that the Crusades conquered.

Notes for Teachers

The Religious Ideology of the Crusades that Lived On

The following hymn could be useful for teachers to help their students to explore the role that the Christian Church played in conquering the lands outside the European Christendom and enslaving peoples who were not Christians. The Christian Church's role in legitimizing the domination and the exploitation of non-Christian people was reflected in religious worship, not only during the period of the Crusades but also during the later phases of European imperialism and the following hymn is an example.

The aim of the following lesson plan is to explore the religious ideology that supported the conquests of the Crusades and to examine the elements of the Crusaders' ideas and thoughts that lived on after them.

Through this lesson students can appreciate that over time some things changed and, others stayed the same. The Hymn 'He shall set up an ensign for the nations' illustrates that, even when the Crusaders stopped conquering the lands of non-Christian peoples, the religious justifications for conquering other lands, developed with the help of the Christian Church, continued during the later period of the European conquests through colonialism. The study of the hymn as an historical source could also be an opportunity for the students to describe the actions and the sentiments of the crusaders and relate these to the religious, social, economic and political gains of the Crusades and the losses of the people conquered.

Students' Work Sheet 2

The following hymn is from a hymn book that was published in 1875. The hymn celebrates the missions of the Crusades centuries after the Crusades and is an example of how some of the ideas of the Crusades were kept alive. The idea of conquering the land of the 'heathens' for a greater cause was useful during the colonial period.

'He shall set up an ensign for the nations'

Lift up your heads, ye gates of brass;
Ye bars of iron, yield;
And let the King of Glory pass;
The Cross is in the field.

That banner, brighter than the star
That leads the train of night,
Shines on the march, and guides from far
His servants to the fight.

A holy war those servants wage;
In that mysterious strife,
The powers of Heav'n and hell engage
For more than death or life.

Ye armies of the living God,
Sworn warriors of Christ's host,
Where hallow'd footsteps never trod,
Take your appointed post.

Though few and small and weak your bands,
Strong in your Captain's strength,
Go to the conquest of all lands:
All must be His at length.

The spoils at His victorious Feet
You shall rejoice to lay,
And lay yourself as trophies meet,
In his great judgement day.

Then fear not, faint not, halt not now;
In Jesus' Name be strong!
To Him shall all the nations bow,
And sing the triumph song:—

Uplifted are the gates of brass,
The bars of iron yield;

Behold the King of Glory pass;
The Cross hath won the field. Amen.
(Hymn no. 586, From Monk, W.H., (1875) *Hymns Ancient and Modern*, London, W. Clowes, p. 835)

Questions

1 From the above hymn, what do you think were the aims of the Crusades?
2 How do you think these aims were achieved?
3 What affect do you think that the Crusades had on the people that they conquered?

Resource Books for Teachers

TREECE, H. (1962) *The Crusades: Two Hundred Years of War, Sacred Journeys and the Quest for Loot*, London, The Souvenir Press.
Cox, D. (1970) *Caste, Class and Race*, New York, Monthly Review Press.

Key Stage Three: Core Study Unit Three

This unit is titled 'The making of the United Kingdom: Crown, Parliament and peoples 1500 to 1750'. One of the sections in this unit is 'changes in ideas and the arts'. Here is a good opportunity for teachers to encourage their students to explore the portrayal of black people in the paintings of this period.

The paintings of this period reflect some of the changes that were taking place in British society as more black people were becoming part of the British society as a result of the slave trade. The paintings depict black people in various occupations as footmen, coachmen, pageboys, soldiers, musicians, actresses, prostitutes, beggars, prisoners, pimps, highway robbers, streetsellers and so on. Dabydeen illustrates that the paintings of this period reflect the exploitation and the oppression of black people in British society. Since the moral justification of the slavery rested largely on the refusal to classify black people as human beings, the dehumanizing of black people is expressed in many ways: pet animals and black people occupied the same peripheral position in the paintings and both the pet animals and the black people were portrayed as viewing their masters with a respectful adoration. Of one such painting by Dandridge 'Young Girl with Dog and Negro Boy', Dabydeen (1987, p. 26) argues that 'a hierarchy of power relationships is being revealed: the superior white (superior in social and human terms) is surrounded by inferior creatures, the black boy and the dog, who share more or less the same status'; he goes on to illustrate that such a painting was one of hundreds. Comparisons between the physiognomy of black people and animals are also made in the paintings of this period as black people are portrayed as resembling animals. In numerous ways, therefore, black people existed in these paintings merely to reflect upon the 'superiority' of the white people. What emerges from such paintings is a sense of loneliness and humiliation of black people in white society.

Dabydeen's illustrative book, *Hogarth's Blacks: Images of Blacks in Eighteenth Century English Art*, is an excellent guide to British paintings during the period of 'The making of the United Kingdom'. The book offers detailed illustrations of paintings and a clear analysis of the social, economic political, religious, cultural and aesthetic forces that moulded the British artists who produced these paintings. Teachers may wish to encourage their students to examine the position of black people in British society as reflected by the painting of the period 1500 to 1750 by studying the paintings clearly reproduced in Dabydeen's book and by visiting an art gallery which has a collection of paintings from this period.

In contrast to the eighteenth century English paintings, teachers may wish to offer their students an opportunity to examine the portrayal of African people in the paintings and stone carvings of the Egyptian civilization of 5000 years ago (Cotterell). The Egyptian artists portrayed their people as intelligent human beings in the process of creating the first human civilization of this world.

Resources for Teachers

Copies of the following paintings are included in Dabydeen's book and are particularly striking in their illustrations of black people in eighteenth century English art.

Wheatley, 'Family Group',
Mingard, 'Duchess of Portsmouth',
Dandridge, 'Young Girl with Dog and Negro Boy',
Riley, 'Charles Seymour — 6th Duke of Somerset',
Van Dyck, 'Henrietta of Lorraine',
Lely, 'Elizabeth Countess of Dysart',
Wright, 'Two Girls and a Negro Servant',
Hamilton, 'Portrait of Young Man with Servant'.

COTTERELL, A. (1980) *The Penguin Encyclopedia of Ancient Civilizations*, London, Penguin.
DABYDEEN, D. (1987) *Hogarth's Blacks: Images of Blacks in Eighteenth-Century English Art*, Manchester, Manchester University Press.

Key Stage Three: Core Study Unit Four

Key Stage Three, 'Expansion, trade and industry: Britain 1750 to 1900', has a section 'patterns of trade with the Empire and other parts of the world'. The following lesson plan aims to offer students an opportunity to examine the essence of Britain's 'trade' with her Empire.

Students' Work Sheet

Britain's Trade in Human Beings

The sixteenth century saw the beginnings of the trade in slaves from Africa to work in the mines and the tobacco, cotton, sugar, coffee and cocoa plantations in the European colonies of America. In terms of profit, slaves were valuable in two ways: as commodities to be traded in and as producers of crops and raw materials.

Several European countries were involved in the buying and selling of African people for slave labour and if we focus on Britain's role in this trade, we find that by the eighteenth century, Britain became the most dominant force in this commerce. Sir John Hawkins transported the first group of 300 slaves from West Africa to the Caribbean island of Hispaniola (now Haiti) in 1562 for Britain. By 1713 under the Treaty of Utrecht, Britain acquired from France the contract to supply African slaves to the Spanish colonies. After this, Britain became the foremost slave carrier and the centre of the triangular trade (Bryan, Dadzie and Scafe, 1985).

Britain was at the centre of the 'triangular trade'. This trade involved buying slaves from Africa with goods produced in Britain, selling slaves in the Caribbean getting the slaves to work without wages on the plantations to produce raw materials, selling the raw materials produced by slave labour in Britain so that the raw materials could be manufactured and used to purchase more slaves.

Activity: Write an account of the triangular slave trade linking the different aspects of social, economic and political development in Britain and the underdevelopment of Western Africa.

Britain's Trade in Cotton Goods

Britain did not have the suitable climate for growing cotton and yet, in the nineteenth century, it became a leading exporters of cotton goods. How was this achieved? One way in which Britain acquired raw cotton was from the slave plantations in the West Indies. This raw cotton was manufactured in the factories of England, Wales and Scotland thereby providing British workers with employment. Britain made enormous profits by selling the finished products in Britain and in many other countries too.

Britain's other source of cotton was its Indian colony. India had a thriving cotton industry and it exported cotton goods to many countries in Asia and Europe long before it was colonized. Under British rule, India's cotton industry was destroyed in the nineteenth century. As rulers of India, Britain forced India to export raw cotton to Britain and to purchase British finished cotton goods. All of this Britain managed to do by developing 'free trade' with India. Free trade was one way trade which allowed free entry for British goods into India, while tariffs were imposed against the entry of Indian goods into Britain. India was also prevented from trading directly with other countries. (Navigation acts which allowed Britain to have free trade were passed and imposed in other British colonies too.)

Between 1814 and 1835, British cotton goods exported to India rose from less than one million yards to over fifty one million yards. In the same period, Indian cotton goods imported into Britain fell from 1,250,000 million pieces to 306,000 pieces and by 1844, to 60,000 pieces. By 1850 India, which for centuries had exported cotton goods to many countries, was importing one fourth of all British goods. This process was carried out through the first half of the nineteenth century and even into the twentieth century (Dutt, 1940).

In this way Britain became a leading manufacturer and supplier of cotton goods and the Indian manufacturing industry was destroyed. For Britain, therefore, India was important as a supplier of raw cotton as well as a market for her goods.

Question: Describe the process by which Britain become a leading manufacturer and supplier of cotton goods during the nineteenth century.

Britain's Trade in Cash Crops

Another route for trade during the days of the British Empire was the cash crop system. In the case of Africa under the cash crop system which was mainly established at the turn of the twentieth century, farmers were forced into producing such crops as cocoa, ground nuts, palm kernels, cotton and coffee for the export market. The cash crops were not grown for the purpose of feeding African people, they were used by the British for trading. Many countries suffered famines after the imposition of the cash crop system under colonial rule. Thus, crops grown on African land with African labour were sold by British traders who fixed the prices and reaped the profits. By paying the labourers low wages, crops were produced cheaply and by selling the produce at high prices in Europe huge profits were made:

> ... the West African Produce Board paid Nigerians £16.15s for a ton of palm oil in 1946 and sold that through the Ministry of Food for £95, which was nearer to the world market prices. Ground nuts which

received £15 per ton bought by the Board were later sold in Britain at £110 per ton. (Rodney, 1972, p. 185)

For the British traders, the cash crop system offered fantastic profits; for the African farmers, indebtedness grew steadily because even the cost of production was not covered by their wages.

Question: How did Britain make profits from the cash crop system?

Project

Discuss the economic, political and social factors that contributed towards Britain's transition from being a leading slave trading nation to being the biggest Empire in the world.

Resource Books for Teachers

DUTT, R.P. (1940) *India Today*, London, Victor Gollancz.
FRYER, P. (1988) *Black People in the British Empire: An Introduction*, London, Pluto Press.
MUKHERJEE, R. (1974) *The Rise and Fall of the East India Company*, London, Monthly Review Press.
RODNEY, W. (1972) *How Europe Underdeveloped Africa*, London, Bogle-L'Ouverture Publications.
SANDWELL DEPARTMENT OF EDUCATION (1987) *Britain and India: An Uncommon Journey*, (Units 1, 2 & 3) Sandwell, Education Development Centre.

Key Stage Three: Core Study Unit Four

The National History Curriculum stipulates that one section of this unit should focus on Britain's world-wide expansion in particular, the expansion of the empire and its impact on the way of life of British people. Here is an excellent opportunity for teachers to help their students to learn about how the British people benefited from Britain's world-wide expansion.

First of all, teachers may wish to discuss with their students some of the economic benefits of colonialism for Britain and her people:

1 The colonies were a source of raw material. (In India the Indian cotton manufacturing industry was destroyed by the British administration, and India was turned into a supplier of raw cotton to Britain);
2 The colonies provided a source of cheap labour. (The farmers, mine workers, etc.);
3 The colonies were used as markets for the manufactured goods. (India was a leading supplier of manufactured cotton in south-east Asia,

but after Britain's intervention, it was turned into an exporter of cotton goods from Britain.)

Secondly, teachers may wish to help their students to explore some of the welfare services (health, social and education) that have been institutionalized in Britain during the last decades of the colonial era. The quality of life of the British people has been greatly improved through the welfare state. Britain was able to provide such extensive welfare support to its people irrespective of the people's ability to pay for them because it was a wealthy country. One of the sources of this wealth was the British Empire. As the governor of the colonies for example, Britain was able to set low prices for the raw materials that were produced in the colonies and sell the finished products that were processed in Britain at high prices. In this way Britain was able to appropriate maximum profits and accumulate wealth. This wealth made a significant contributions towards the development of Britain including its institutions such as the welfare services. World wide expansion through colonialism therefore brought employment and prosperity to the people of Britain and teachers could set their students a project which aimed to explore this process explicitly.

Project

Finally, teachers may wish to help their students to examine the ideological impact of the British Empire on the people of Great Britain. A general misconception among the people of imperial nations is that their ancestors played an enlightening role during their colonial mission, and the general British public is no exception. Students could carry out a survey to find out what the adults in their communities believe was Britain's role in the education of the people of its colonies. Do the adults that the students are surrounded by believe that Britain was a carrier of civilization to the countries it governed? Do they believe that Britain played a less than positive educational role in its colonies? Once the surveys have been carried out, students could share their findings through a structured group discussion. Teachers may also wish to use the following quote which offers a colonized people's perspective on the education provided by their colonizers. For thirteen and fourteen year-old-students, this quote provides an interesting opportunity for role play.

Students' Work Sheet

The Role of Colonial Education

A is sitting on B. A is carried, fed and clothed by B. What kind of education will A want B to get? ... A will want to educate B to obscure the fact that it is B who is carrying, feeding and clothing A. A will want B to learn the philosophy which says the world does not change. A will want to teach B the religion which tells him that the present situation is divinely willed and nothing can be done about it, or that B is in the present plight because he has sinned, or that B should endure his lot because in heaven he will get plenty. Religion, any religion, is very useful to A, for it teaches that the situation in which A is sitting on B is not brought about by man; it is not historical: on the contrary, it's a natural law of the universe, sanctioned by God. A will want B to believe that he, B, has no culture or his culture is inferior. A will then want B to imbibe a culture that inculcates in him values of self-doubt, self-denigration, in a word, a slave consciousness. (Wa Thiong'o, 1983, p. 92)

Group A:
Do a role play about the life-style of A.

Group B:
Do a role play about the education that A is offering to B.

Group C:
Do a role play about the religion that A is trying to teach B.

Group D:
Do a role play about the type of culture that A wants B to adopt.

Group E:
Do a role play about B challenging and resisting A's rule over B.

Notes for Teachers

The teacher may wish to make links between race oppression and gender oppression. The following quotes may be useful for this purpose. The quotes are from 'The female animal: Medical and biological views of woman and her role in nineteenth-century America', by Smith-Rosenberg, C. and Rosenberg, C., in Caplan, A.L., Engelhardt, H.T. and McCartney, J.J. (Eds) 1981, *Concepts of Health and Disease, Interdisciplinary Perspectives*, USA, Addison-Wesley.

Woman is to deal with domestic affections and uses, not with philosophies and sciences. . . . She is priest not king. The house, the chamber, the closet, are the centres of her social life and power, as surely as the sun is the centre of the solar system. (Caplan *et al.*, 1981, p. 286)

...but it is better that the future matrons of the state should be without a University training than that it should be produced at the fearful expense of ruined health; better that the future mothers of the state should be robust, hearty, healthy women, than that, by over-study, they entail upon their descendants the germs of disease. (Caplan *et al.*, 1981, p. 290)

The areas of study outlined in the lesson plan covering the expansion of the British Empire and its impact on the economy and way of life of the British people offers students an opportunity to investigate different patterns of change, examine different types of cause and consequence, and analyse and compare the ideas, beliefs and attitudes of people in the British Empire through the examination of the impact of British rule on its colonies.

Resource Books for Teachers

CAPLAN, A.L., ENGELHARDT, H.T. and McCARTNEY, J.J. (Eds) (1981) *Concepts of Health and Disease, Interdisciplinary perspectives*, USA, Addison-Wesley.
PORTER, B. (1984) *The Lion's Share, A Short History of British Imperialism 1850–1983*, London, Longman.
RODNEY, W. (1972) *How Europe Underdeveloped Africa*, London, Bogle-L'Ouverture Publications.
WA THIONG'O, N. (1983) *Barrel of a Pen*, London, New Beacon Books.
SANDWELL DEPARTMENT OF EDUCATION (1987) *Britain and India: An Uncommon Journey*, (Units 1, 2 & 3) Sandwell, Education Development Centre.

Key Stage Three: Core Study Unit Five

The era of the Second World War is the title of this unit; it has a sub-section, 'the legacy of the First World War'. The following lesson plan aims to examine the short and long term impact of the First World War on Britain and its Empire.

Students' Work Sheet

The Legacy of the First World War

The people of the British Empire did not look upon Britain as their caring guardian for Britain was their colonizer. As colonized people, they had witnessed their countries' wealth and resources being plundered by Britain. Thus the people of the British Empire saw Britain as their enemy.

The people of the British Empire fought against their colonizer from the first day that the colonials stepped foot on their rich soil. At the turn of the twentieth century, Britain was finding it more and more difficult to hold its empire together. Then Britain gained new enemies. This time it was not the people that it colonized, it was the people of another European country which became jealous of the size of Britain's empire. Britain had the largest empire in the world and Germany, another European imperial nation had a much smaller empire. Since much of the accessible world had been carved up and colonized by the western European nations, the only way of expanding their empires was for the European imperial nations to fight each other for new colonies. And so, the First World War was started. As Porter explains:

> The Great War when it came was no surprise to imperialists, who had been expecting something like it for years. It stood to reason that the period when European nations could expand freely was coming to an end, that there would soon be no more unclaimed territory to expand into, and that the only way left to expand would be at other European nations' expense. The country which stood to lose most when this colonial rivalry turned cannibalistic was Britain, because she had most colonial flesh on her. It was becoming equally obvious that Germany was the rival most likely to threaten her: the Great Power whose colonial appetite had been least satisfied over the past thirty years, and the one whose face recently had carried the hungriest and most bellicose expression. (Porter, 1984, p. 233)

Question: Why was Britain the enemy of the people of its empire?

Britain Goes to War

Those British people who were against their country being an imperial nation as well as many people of the British Empire believed that one of the aims, of Britain going to war was to preserve its empire. This perspective on the First World War has been documented by some European historians such as Porter and third-world historians such as Rodney. This is not the popular understanding of the cause of the First World War.

The resistance of the colonized people against their oppressor was becoming increasingly difficult for Britain to contain and so, in some ways, the rivalry expressed by Germany against Britain was almost a gift. Britain portrayed Germany as a threat to world peace and dragged the people of its empire to fight against its enemy. By doing so, Britain hoped to divert the attention of the people of the colonies. It was in Britain's interest not to be viewed as the enemy by the people of its empire. It was in Britain's interest to get the people of its empire to unite and fight on behalf of Britain against Britain's enemy. Some British people believed that the war 'achieved a greater measure of effective imperial unity in its direction than statesmen had ever contemplated before' (Porter, 1984, p. 237).

However, in spite of this forced unity, the people in the British colonies never really lost sight of who their enemy really was. They were conscious of thousands of their people being forced to go to war, a war that they did not believe in. They were conscious of thousands of their people being killed in a war that they were not responsible for. Altogether two and a half million colonials fought for Britain and thousands more served as non-combatants. The number of people from the colonies and the dominions that were killed in the First World War were:

62,056	Indians
59,330	Australians
57,843	Canadians
16,711	New Zealanders
7,121	South Africans
2,000	East Africans
850	West Africans (Porter, 1984, p. 235)

The people in the colonies were also conscious of the enormous amount of wealth that was drained out of their countries for the war effort. Many colonies had to make direct grants of money and the other colonies had to supply material goods. As Churchill explained to the House of Commons after the war:

the commodities which they [the colonies] produced were in many cases vital to the maintenance of the industries, and particularly the war industries, of Britain and her Allies. (Porter, 1984, p. 236)

Question: What effect did the First World War have on the colonies of the British Empire?

The Legacy of the War

Britain won the war with the help of the people of its great empire and Germany who had a much smaller empire lost the war. And because Germany lost the war, it lost its empire too. Britain acquired numerous 'mandate' territories. These mandate territories 'were entrusted to Britain by the League of Nations to administer in the interests of their inhabitants, and with a view to their eventual independence. However, the British ministers did not treat their new mandate territories, when they got them, any differently from their existing colonies' (Porter, 1984, p. 249).

Figure 8: Indian soldiers in Europe during the First World War.

The conditions of 1919 determined that, initially, Britain would get a great deal out of the war for herself. In the first place, she and her allies had won the war, and Germany and Turkey had lost. This meant that there were, suddenly, a large number of colonies going begging in the world ... Consequently the first result of the war for Britain was a considerable augmentation of her empire. The middle east was divided up ... The Arabs for their efforts were given the Arabian desert. Britain took for herself Palestine, Transjordon, the Persian Gulf states and Iraq: which together with her existing protectorates in Egypt, Cyprus and Aden made up a tidy little middle eastern empire.... Britain took Tanganyika from Germany ... In the west of Africa the Gold Coast and Nigeria were extended at the expense of parts of Togoland and the Cameroons, and further down the Union of South Africa took over the administration of South-West Africa. With Britain's colonies remaining intact despite the disruption of the past four years, and all these additions, the British empire in 1919 was more extensive than it had ever been. (Porter, 1984, p. 249)

The peace that followed the First World War was costly for the people that were killed in Europe and the countries of the European empires. And while Britain won the war and gained new colonial territories, its grip on its old empire weakened. The people of the British colonies were not blind, they had not lost sight of who their enemy was. So, once again, the people of the British Empire challenged their oppressor in every way that they could and many took up arms against their foreign rulers. For Britain, this was the legacy of the First World War.

Vocabulary

imperial	plantations
exploit	colonies
oppress	resistance
invade	legacy

Activity: Do a project giving an example of each of the above from the history of Britain.

Resource Books for Teachers

PORTER, B. (1984) *The Lion's Share: A Short History of British Imperialism 1850–1983*, London, Longman.

SANDWELL DEPARTMENT OF EDUCATION (1987) *Britain and India: An Uncommon Journey*, (Unit 1) Sandwell, Education Development Centre.
RODNEY, W. (1972) *How Europe Underdeveloped Africa*, London, Bogle-L'ouverture Publications.

Key Stage Three: Supplementary Unit A

One of the Supplementary Units for Key Stage 3 is 'Culture and society in Ireland from early times to the beginning of the twentieth century'. This is a controversial area of British history and most of the information available on this subject tends to have a British rather than an Irish perspective. For this reason, the following lesson plan aims to offer an Irish perspective on the culture and society in Ireland. The following information on the history of Ireland has been drawn from the work of historians who write with an Irish perspective, for example Irish women writers in 'Women in Struggle', 1978, De Baroid, 1989, Beckett, 1966 and Lyons, 1971 and 1979.

Students' Work Sheet

Introduction

The relationship that Britain has had with Ireland for over 500 years has affected the socio-economic and cultural organization of Ireland historically and today. It is necessary therefore to examine this relationship in detail when studying the culture and society of Ireland from early times to the beginning of the twentieth century.

Exercise 1: The Social and Economic Organization of Ireland Prior to its Colonization

Before colonization, Ireland was a country with its own culture, religion, social customs and language. The Irish people lived in small groups (clans) which consisted of several families. The land did not belong to any individual but belonged to the community as a whole. Most of the Irish people lived by farming the land, rearing livestock or hunting. Everyone was not equal in the Irish society for the kings, chiefs and priests were richer and had more power than the farmers and the hunters. The relationship between women and men was not one of equality either, for men had the right to marry more than one wife. However, women were entitled to inherit and own property, they had the right to vote in popular assemblies and could be elected to the position of chief. Irish law had also established well-defined rights for women in cases of separation, divorce, etc.

Question: What were the characteristics of the Irish society before the co-lonization of Ireland?

Exercise 2: The English Conquest of Ireland

England began to conquer Ireland from the fifth century onwards. In the twelfth century, substantial areas of Ireland were colonized by England and by the sixteenth century, Ireland was fully subjected to English rule. The clan system of small groups of people living together and supporting each other was broken down as a new English system of living and working was imposed on Ireland.

The English conquest had a destructive effect on the Irish society: the relationship that the Irish people traditionally had with their land was changed drastically. All Irish land had to be surrendered to the English Crown, and then the land was rented to English settlers or to clan chiefs. The majority of the people of Ireland were turned into tenant farmers or labourers and reduced to a state of poverty and destitution. In this way, the majority of the Irish people did not benefit from the fruits of their labour for the greatest profits were reaped by the English.

The English colonization of Ireland also changed the social and eco-nomic position of the Irish women. Whereas under the Celtic Law, which existed in Ireland before it was colonized by England, women were entitled to inherit property, the English law allowed only the eldest male child to inherit property. With no rights to land or property the position of women was weakened dramatically. The majority of the Irish people were Catholic. The English and the Scottish people who went to Ireland were Protestants. The English law that was imposed in Ireland also limited the inheritance rights of Catholic men and denied them all civil and political rights. Further-more, Catholic people were deprived of the right to vote in their own par-liament, forbidden to join the army, and to practice or teach the Catholic religion.

Question: What were the consequences of colonization for Ireland?

Exercise 3: The Repression of the Irish People

During the seventeenth century English rule faced a major revolt in Ireland, and England retaliated ruthlessly. Many Irish lords who resisted English rule were driven from their land and hundreds of peasants and labouring people who rebelled were massacred or sold as slaves by the English government. Nevertheless, by the late seventeenth century England's attempt to drive out the Irish and to plant the country with English and Scots settlers was greatly undermined by the resistance of the Irish people.

Question: What happened to the Irish people who fought against their country being colonized?

Exercise 4: The Partition of Ireland

Today's situation in Ireland can be traced to England's sixteenth and seventeenth century colonial policies. The greatest number of English and Scottish people settled in the north of Ireland. Here the agricultural economy was changed by the English and Scottish settlers to an industrial one, and Ulster became a centre for the linen trade while the rest of the Irish economy was neglected.

England's colonial policies in Ireland eventually resulted in a British colony in the north and the underdevelopment of the rest of Ireland. Colonialism also forced many landless and unemployed Irish people to leave their country and search for employment in other countries. Families were divided as the men emigrated to America, England, Scotland and to Wales.

Question: Some people tell jokes about the Irish immigrants. How would you explain the history of the Irish immigrants to such a person?

Exercise 5: Ireland's Struggle Against British Rule

The uneven development of Ireland contributed towards Ireland's uneven struggle against its colonizers. By the nineteenth century, there was a widespread nationalist political movement in the Catholic south where the clergy, the urban elite and the peasantry were seeking radical land reform and complete independence from Britain. In contrast, in Ulster, where the industries were dependent on the British link, a sectarian opposition to Home Rule developed. This is where a movement in favour of preserving union with Britain grew.

Britain attempted to resolve this conflict by dividing Ireland, and a 'partition' between northern and southern Ireland was formally introduced in 1921. Six of the nine counties of Ulster, with a protestant majority, formed the Northern Ireland State. One of the aims of this solution was to enable Britain to maintain economic and political control of the most industrially developed part of Ireland.

Explain the Following Terms:

1 Nationalist politics;
2 Sectarian opposition;
3 Home Rule;

Figure 9: The colonial partition of Ireland: Donegal, Monaghan and Cavan, formerly part of Ulster, were removed at the time of partition in order to ensure a Protestant, pro-British majority in Northern Ireland. Donegal in the north of Ireland is therefore part of Southern Ireland.

4 Partition;
5 Economic and political control.

Teacher's Notes

Once the students have worked through the above work sheet, they should have some understanding about Ireland's history. With an awareness of this historical perspective, the students will be better able to comprehend the present situation in Ireland. Interestingly, the National Curriculum expects teachers to teach about the culture and society in Ireland only up to the beginning of this century. Why is this so? Why does this government not wish teachers to teach their students about the situation in Ireland, at least up to 'circa twenty years ago' as recommended in the other units? The government may have its own objectives for including certain histories and excluding others in the National Curriculum. Teachers may wish to use imaginative ways of offering their students a balanced history within the framework imposed by the government. The following study plan is offered as an example:

Students' Work Sheet

Group A:
Do a role play about family life in pre-colonial Ireland.

Group B:
Do a role play about family life in seventeenth century Ireland under the British rule.

Group C:
Do a role play about one Irish family's struggle during the potato famine.

Group D:
Do a role play about the life of an Irish family which emigrated to America during the potato famine.

Group E:
In some families, only the men emigrated, hoping to support their families by finding employment overseas. Do a role play about the life of the remaining members of such a family.

Group F:
Do a role play about one Irish family's struggle against British rule.

Group G:
The following is a list of the civilians who were killed in the small Ballymurphy community of Belfast in 1971 (about twenty years ago):

Fr Hugh Mullan (37) by British Army, August 9th 1971;
Frank Quinn (20) by British Army, August 9th 1971;
Joan Connolly (50) by British Army, August 9th 1971;
Daniel Teggart (44) by British Army, August 9th 1971;
Noel Phillips (20) by British Army, August 9th 1971;
Eddie Doherty (28) by British Army, August 10th 1971;
John Lavery (19) by British Army, August 10th 1971;
Paddy McCarthy (44) stress of internment week, August 11th 1971;
John McKerr of Andersonstown, by unknown pro-British gunmen, possibly
    soldiers, August 11th 1971;
Joseph Murphy (41) by British Army, August 22nd 1971;
Joseph Corr (43) by British Army, August 27th 1971;
Thomas McIlroy (29) by British Army, February 2nd 1972;
Tommy McIlroy (50) of Andersonstown, by loyalists, May 13th 1972;
Robert McMullan (32) by loyalists or British Army, May 13th 1972;
Martha Campbell (13) by loyalists, May 14th 1972;
John Moran (19) of Turf Lodge, by loyalists, May 23rd 1972;
James Bonner (19) of Iveagh, by British Army, June 25th 1972;
Bernard Norney (38) by IRA, June 27th 1972;
Margaret Gargan (13) by British Army, July 9th 1972;
Fr Noel Fitzpatrick (40) by British Army, July 9th 1972;
Paddy Butler (38) by British Army, July 9th 1972;
David McCaffrey (14) by British Army, July 9th 1972;
Patrick McKee (25) by loyalists, September 30th 1972;
Jimmy Gillen (21) by loyalists, October 18th 1972.
(De Baroid, 1989)

Do a role play about a family in Northern Ireland as it tries to cope with one
of its members being killed in the war.

Teacher's Notes

An interesting aspect of the Irish culture is the impact of religion on its
people, particularly its women members. This could also be explored in this
unit.

> 'Irish women's position today has its roots in the colonial history and
> the survival of religion as the dominant ideology. For in Ireland,
> unlike the advanced Western nations where the transition from feu-
> dalism to capitalism ensured the subordination of ideology (religion)
> to the economic, the transition was not internally generated but
> externally imposed. Britain nurtured the Irish feudal classes in order
> to undermine the rise of an indigenous capitalism, and one of the
> results has been the continuation of these old classes and in particu-
> lar their ideologies. (*Women in Struggle*, 1978, p. 28)

Divorce, abortion, contraceptives, homosexuality and the laws relating to married women's property rights are some areas that could be examined.

Resource Books for Teachers

DE BAROID, C. (1989) *Ballymurphy and the Irish War*, Baile Atha Cliath 4, Aisling Publishers.
BECKETT, J.C. (1966) The Making of Modern Ireland 1603–1923, London, Faber.
LYONS, F.S.L. (1971) Ireland Since the Famine, London, Fontana.
LYONS, F.S.L. (1979) Culture and Anarchy in Ireland 1890–1939, Oxford, Oxford University Press.
'Women in Struggle' (1978) London, Rising Free Bookshop.

Key Stage Three: Supplementary Unit C

For Key Stage Three Supplementary Unit entitled, 'Black peoples of the Americas: 16th to early 20th centuries', the National Curriculum Council (1991) offers a useful teaching plan. It suggests that pupils could be introduced to the experiences of black Americans in the Caribbean and the USA and that the focus could be on slavery, emancipation and the forging of new identities and cultures. The Council also suggests that the content could include information on the slave economy, the resistance and emancipation of the slaves, segregation and discrimination of black people after emancipation and the continued struggle for equality (National Curriculum Council, 1991, F36). The following two lesson plans are offered as part of this unit.

The aim of the first study plan is to focus on the emancipation of the slaves. The study plan also offers an opportunity to gain an insight into the process by which people remember certain elements of their history and are not aware of other parts of their history.

The aim of the second study plan is to focus on the vital link between the European trade in human beings and the development of a racist ideology for the justification of this trade. This study plan also offers an opportunity to examine the ideas, beliefs and attitudes of a group of people holding a privileged position in society in the nineteenth century.

Students' Work Sheet 1

Slave Resistance and Rebellions

Slave resistance started on board the ships that took the slaves to the New World. The slaves rebelled against their captors on the ships even though

Figure 10: The slaves of St Dominique led by Toussaint L'ouverture defeat the colonialists. Central to the abolition of slavery was the resistance which the slaves put up. The successful slave revolution in St Dominique sent a shock wave through Europe.

they were severely punished for doing so. There were numerous cases of individual defiance as slaves chose to jump off the ship and drown rather than be oppressed and degraded through slavery.

Once the slaves arrived in the Americas, their struggle for liberation intensified. Many slaves ran away and formed communities, 'maroons' in the dense forests. Some Maroons pursued a life of freedom, and other Maroons chose to wage a war against the slavers. Women, men and children from the Maroons joined in this fight. Nanny of Maroon Town was one such guerilla fighter. Nanny was renowned for her skills in organizing and directing campaigns during the Maroon Wars using the 'abeng' (maroon horn) to communicate messages from one group of guerillas to the next. Cubah, 'Queen of Kingston', was another African woman freedom fighter who fought against slavery. Cubah played a central role in plotting a massive uprising in Jamaica in 1760. When the plot was discovered, Cubah was deported to another island, although she soon returned to continue her struggle against the slavers. Cubah was finally captured and executed.

While many slaves who ran away joined the Maroons, other runaway slaves tried to survive in towns by doing odd jobs or by taking up fishing or woodcutting. Within the plantations, opposition ranged from the burning of the fields or the plantation buildings, poisoning of the planters, sabotage, working slowly, pretending not to understand the slavers and developing ways of communicating which the slavers could not understand.

Black women who worked as domestic slaves found their own ways of resisting their oppressors. Their acts ranged from daring attempts to poison the food consumed by the household to using their access to books and newspapers to teach themselves to read and write in secret, thus becoming a source of news and information to fellow slaves. These activities were particularly significant, since every effort was made to prevent slaves from learning to read or write. Such acts were truly courageous, for all forms of subversion, whether overt or covert, were punished with equal force if detected. Corporal and capital punishment were a well-entrenched feature of slavery. The power to terrorize and intimidate kept the system of slavery going as long as it did.

Group Activity

In groups of five or six, do a role play about the struggles of resistance of the slaves against the slavers.

Notes for Teachers

In the nineteenth century, slavery was outlawed, primarily because slave rebellions rendered slavery uneconomic and Britain instituted a new, more economic form of slavery, namely the indenture labour system (see Chapter 2 and also, Tinker, 1974). At this time also, Britain was extending her empire rapidly. Having destroyed huge communities of people in Australia, New Zealand and Tasmania, Britain began to consolidate imperial rule in these and other countries of this world. Many British people know about the termination of slavery, and they believe that slavery was outlawed merely because of the growth of humanitarianism within Britain. Not many British people know, however, about Britain's indenture labour system or the destructive policies of the British Empire. Teachers may wish to help their students to do a survey among the adults that surround them and ask them key questions about Britain's role in slavery, Britain's role in the emancipation of the slaves, Britain's role in the indenture labour system and Britain's role in the colonies. The findings could be interesting material for discussing questions such as what history is taught in British schools and why?

Students' Work Sheet 2

The following are quotes from the 'Report on the Diseases and Physical Peculiarities of the Negro Race' by Samuel A. Cartwright, *The New Orleans Medical and Surgical Journal* (May, 1851): pp. 691–715, lately published in Caplan, A.L., Engelhardt, H.T. and McCartney, J.J. (Eds) 1981, *Concepts of Health and Disease, Interdisciplinary Perspectives,* USA, Addison-Wesley.

Exercise 1: Religious Justification for Slavery

We learn from the Book of Genesis, that Noah had three sons, Shem, Ham and Japhet, and that Canaan, the son of Ham, was doomed to be servant of servants unto his brethren. From history, we learn that the descendants of Canaan settled in Africa, and are the present Ethiopians, or black race of men. . . . (Cartwright, 1851 in Caplan, *et. al.*, 1981, p. 310)

Question: This writer believed that black people are supposed to be the descendants of Canaan and therefore should be slaves and servants. What do you think?

Exercise 2: White Slavers' Perceptions of African People

Before African people were enslaved, they lived in various forms of communities: small, self-sufficient agricultural and hunting groups, small village communities with social and economic structures, larger towns with more complex social, economic, social and political systems and large city states with

sophisticated structures of government. These various communities were expressions of great intelligence and creativity. Nevertheless, the slavers chose
to look upon the slaves as unintelligent children. In so doing, the slavers
avoided guilt feelings that most human beings would have if they were to
treat other human beings with so much cruelty.

> Although their skin is very thick, it is as sensitive, when they are in
> perfect health, as that of children, and like them they fear the rod.
> They resemble children in another very important particular, they
> are very easily governed by love combined with fear, and are ungov-
> ernable, vicious and rude under any other form of government
> .... Like children it is not necessary that they be kept under the fear
> of the lash; it is sufficient that they be kept under the fear of offend-
> ing those who have authority over them. Like children they require
> government in every thing; food, clothing, exercise, sleep all require
> to be prescribed by rule, or they will run into excesses. Like children,
> they are apt to over-eat themselves or to confine their diet too much
> to one favourite article, unless restrained from doing so. (Cartwright,
> 1851, in Caplan *et. al.*, 1981, p. 309)

Question: Why did this writer believe that African people are like children?

Exercise 3: The Slavers' Perception of the Resistance of the Slaves

The slaves rebelled against their oppressors in many ways. Some chose to run
away, others chose not to work hard or to burn down slaver's buildings and
so forth. Instead of seeing such actions as signs of resistance, many slavers
believed that these were signs of sickness and therefore needed treatment. In
this way, the slavers once again masked the truth because it suited them.

> Drapetomania [from two Greek words meaning], a runaway slave,
> and mad or crazy. It is unknown to our medical authorities, although
> its diagnostic symptom, the absconding from service, is well known
> to our planter and overseers, as it was to the ancient Greeks ... The
> cause, in the most of cases, that induces the negro to run away from
> service, is as much a disease of the mind as any other species of
> mental alienation, and much more curable, as a general rule. With
> the advantages of proper medical advice, strictly followed, this trou-
> blesome practice that many negroes have of running away, can be
> almost entirely prevented.... (Cartwright, 1851, in Caplan *et al.*, 1981,
> p. 318)

Question: Why did this writer believe that the slaves who ran away were sick?

Exercise 4: The Slavers' Justification for Physically Abusing the Slaves

The slavers punished the slaves in numerous ways. Slaves were whipped for the slightest reasons for refusing to participate in the great load of work that was imposed upon them. Such treatment by one group of human beings against another was justified in many ways and the following is one example.

> Before negroes run away, unless they are frightened or panicstruck, they become sulky and dissatisfied. The cause of this sulkiness and dissatisfaction should be inquired into and removed, or they are apt to run away. . . . When sulky and dissatisfied without cause, the experience of those on the line and elsewhere was decidedly in favour of whipping them out of it, as a preventive measure against absconding or other bad conduct. It was called whipping the devil out of them. (Cartwright, 1851, in Caplan *et al.*, 1981, p. 320)

Other ways of controlling the slaves was to 'treat them kindly'. This involved taking away the slaves' rights to socialize with their sisters, brothers, relatives and friends and making sure that the slaves did not work for more than eight to ten hours a day. This the slavers believed was treating the slaves with 'care, kindness, attention and humanity' (Cartwright, 1851, in Caplan *et al.*, 1981, p. 322).

> If treated kindly, well fed and clothed, with fuel enough to keep a small fire burning all night, separated into families, each family having its own house — not permitted to run about at night, or visit their neighbours, or to receive visits, or to use intoxicating liquors, and not overworked or exposed too much to the weather, they are easily governed — more so than any other people in the world. . . . They have only to be kept in that state, and treated like children, with care, kindness, attention and humanity, to prevent and cure them from running away. (Cartwright, 1851, in Caplan *et al.*, 1981, p. 320)

Question: Many slave owners whipped the slaves to stop them from running away. What does this writer consider to be the best way of looking after the slaves?

Exercise 5: The Slavers' Perception of the Slaves Continued Resistance

Many slaves were not deterred by the physical violence that the white men meted out to them, and they resolutely continued their campaigns of resistance. Some slavers chose to see the continued liberation struggles of the slaves as manifestations of illness.

Dysaesthesia Aethiopis is a disease peculiar to negroes. . . . From the careless movements of the individuals affected with the complaint, they are apt to do much mischief, which appears as if intentional, but is mostly owing to the stupidity of mind and insensibility of the nerves induced by the disease. Thus, they break, waste and destroy everything they handle — abuse horses and cattle — tear, burn or rend their own clothing, and paying no attention to the rights of property, they steal other's to replace what they have destroyed . . . . The disease is the natural offspring of negro liberty — the liberty to be idle, to wallow in filth, and to indulge in improper food and drinks.

When aroused from his sloth by the stimulus of hunger, he takes anything he can lay his hands on, and tramples on the rights as well as on the property of others, with perfect indifference as to consequences. When driven to labour by the compulsive power of the white man, he performs the task assigned him in a headlong, careless manner, treading down with his feet, or cutting with his hoe the plants he is put to cultivate — breaking the tools he works with, and spoiling everything he touches that can be injured by careless handling. Hence the overseers call it 'rascality', supposing that the mischief is intentionally done. But there is no premeditated mischief in the case — the mind is too torpid to meditate mischief . . .
(Cartwright, 1851, in Caplan *et al.*, 1981, p. 222)

Question: Many slaves fought against their slavers. Some refused to work, others burned down the farms and many ran away. Do you think that the slaves who fought against their slaver were sick?

Exercise 6: The Treatment of Slaves Who Rebelled Constantly

The complaint is easily curable, if treated on sound physiology principles. The skin is dry, thick and harsh to the touch and the liver inactive. The liver, skin and kidneys should be stimulated to activity, and be made to assist in decarbonising the blood. The best means to stimulate the skin is, first, to have the patient well washed with warm water and soap; then, to anoint it all over with oil, and to slap the oil in with a broad leather strap; then to put the patient to some hard kind of work in the open air and sunshine, that will compel him to expand his lungs, as chopping wood, splitting rails or sawing . . . After a moderate meal, he should resume his work again, resting at intervals, and taking refreshments. . . . At night he should be lodged in a warm room with a small fire in it, and should have a clean bed, with sufficient blanket covering, and be washed clean before going to bed; in the morning, oiled, slapped and put to work as before. Such treatment will, in a short time, effect a cure in all cases which are not complicated with chronic visceral derangements. No sooner does the blood feel the vivifying influences derived from its full and perfect atmospherization . . . then the negro seems to be awakened to a new existence, and to look thankful and grateful to the white man whose compulsory power, by making him inhale vital air, has restored his sensation and dispelled the mist that clouded his intellect. (Cartwright, 1851, in Caplan *et al.*, 1981, pp. 320–324)

Question: How did some slave owners treat slaves that rebelled constantly?

Exercise 7: European Benefits from Slavery

The Europeans who benefited from the slave trade and the slave plantations were not blind to their gains from slavery even though they tried to turn a blind eye to their inhumanity against the enslaved African peoples.

The compulsory power of the white man, by making the slothful negro take active exercise, puts into active play the lungs, through whose agency the vitalized blood is sent to the brain, to give liberty to the mind, and to open the door to intellectual improvement. The very exercise, so beneficial to the negro, is expended in cultivating those burning fields in cotton, sugar, rice and tobacco, which, but for his labour, would from the heat of the climate, go uncultivated, and their products lost to the world. Both parties are benefited — the negro as well as his master — even more. But there is a third party benefited — the world at large. The three millions of bales of cotton, made by negro labour, afford a cheap clothing for the civilized world. The labouring classes of all mankind, having less to pay for clothing, have more money to spend in educating their children, and in intellectual, moral and religious progress. (Cartwright, 1851, in Caplan *et al.*, 1981, p. 324)

Question: In what ways does this writer believe that the African people benefited from being slaves?
Do you think that the African people benefited from slavery?
According to this writer, how did the Europeans benefit from slavery?

Exercise 8: Written Work

Describe the living conditions of the African slaves in the Caribbean.

Resource Books for Teachers

BRYAN, B., DADZIE, S., SCAFE, S. (1985) *The Heart of the Race: Black women's Lives in Britain*, London, Virago.

CAPLAN, A.L., ENGELHARDT, H.T. and McCARTNEY, J.J. (Eds) (1981) *Concepts of Health and Disease, Interdisciplinary Perspectives*, Addison-Wesley.

GENOVESE, E. (1974) *Roll Jordan Roll: The World the Slaves Made*, New York, Pantheon.

HART, R. (1985) *Slaves Who Abolished Slavery: Blacks in Rebellion*, (Volume 2), Jamaica, Institute of Social and Economic Research.

TINKER, H. (1974) *A New System of Slavery: The Export of Indian Labour Overseas, 1830–1920*, London, Open University Press.

Key Stage Three: Supplementary Unit C

This Supplementary Units covers the study of several groups of non-European people, for example, the indigenous peoples of North America.

Taking into account the requirements of the National Curriculum, the following study plan aims to examine the key historical issues concerning the people of North America.

Students' Work Sheet

Exercise 1: The First Nation People of America

Many Cowboy and Indian films portray the first nation peoples of America (often referred to as American Indians) as backward savages who attacked the God-fearing, peace-loving and highly civilized European settlers.

The following extract explains that far from being backward, the first nation people of America lived in well organized communities. The people of these communities aimed at living peacefully with each other. They shared the food that they produced equally among themselves, thus preventing some people from becoming privileged while others starved. Women played an important role in the community: they were not treated only as bearers of children and carers of families. Some of the communities in which the indigenous American people lived were big, covering vast areas of land and many different ethnic groups of people. For this to be possible, complex social, economic and political systems were needed. All of this did not involve a small group of people organizing life for the rest of the people. All the people of the community had a say in how their lives would be run. This is an example of true democracy:

Figure 11: The First Nation People of North America have a long history of living communally in harmony with nature.

As on the three other major continental land masses of the world, civilization in America emerged from certain centres, . . . with periods of vigorous growth and integration, as well as decline and disintegration. At least a dozen such centres were functioning when the Europeans intervened. In North America, a remarkable federal state structure had incorporated five widely dispersed nations of thousands of agricultural villages. This was the Iroquois Confederacy originally comprising five nations. . . . The Confederacy was a highly structured state system which allowed the multi-ethnic state to incorporate peoples and nations. . . . The remarkable aspect of the Iroquois state was its ability to avoid centralisation by means of a clan-village system of democracy, based on collective ownership of the land; its products, stored in granaries, were distributed equitable to the people by elected authorities. 'Clan mothers' played the key role of supervising all activities, having the final veto on any decision. (Dunbar Ortiz, 1984, p. 2)

Activity: Describe the social organisation of the Iroquois Confederacy of North America.

Exercise 2: The Oppression of the First Nation People

Today the descendants of the first nation peoples of North America have few rights to their land and the majority of them live in poverty:

The 4th World is the name given to the indigenous peoples descended from a country's aboriginal population and who today are completely or partly deprived of the right to their own territory and its riches. The peoples of the 4th World have only limited influence or none at all in the national state to which they belong. The peoples to whom we refer are the Indians of North and South America, the Inuit (Eskimos), the Sami people, the Australian aborigines, as well as various indigenous populations in Africa, Asia and Oceania.

The oppression of aboriginal populations assumes many forms. It ranges from a general lack of understanding and disrespect for non-European culture and life-style and may go as far as the kind of oppression which, in many countries, means a cultural and, in certain areas, outright physical extermination. (Dunbar Ortiz, 1984, p. 82)

Explain the Following Terms:

First nation peoples/Indigenous people
The first world

Figure 12: Bhattra women in India demand for their community the right to live in the forests where their ancestors lived. The banner says that 'we want pristine forests'.

Figure 13: Ngaanyatjaura Land Rights meeting.
Australian aborigines gathered to demand the freedom to cultivate and live in the Gibson desert, Western Australia.

The second world
The third world
The fourth world

Exercise 3: Research for Students

Reading List:

INSTITUTE OF RACE RELATIONS (1982) Book One, *Roots of Racism* — Chapter four: Colonisation.
INSTITUTE OF RACE RELATIONS (1982) Book Two, *Patterns of Racism* — Chapter two: Countries of large scale European settlement.

Activity: The first nation peoples of North America have been herded into reservations, miserable and barren areas of land in their own country. On the reservations, they live in extreme poverty with poor housing, education and health facilities. Survival International is a world wide movement to support first nation people. It stands for their right to decide their own future and help them to protect their lands, environment and way of life. Write to Survival International, 310 Edgware Road, London, W2 1DY. (Telephone 071 723 5535) for information about the struggles and the resistance of the first nation peoples of North America.

Resource Books for Teachers

BURGER, J. (1987) *Report From the Frontier: The State of the World's Indigenous Peoples*, London, Zed Press.
DUNBAR ORTIZ, R. (1984) *Indians of the Americas: Human Rights and Self Determination*, London, Zed Press.

Key Stage Four: Core Study Unit

Key stage Four requires teachers to teach their students about the 'reasons for the break-up of the overseas empires of European countries'. The Indian war of independence is an interesting case study of the beginning of the break-up of the British empire. It is also a good example of how history is recorded with numerous perspectives.

The following lesson plan has been designed for fifteen to sixteen year old students. The aims of this lesson are:

1   To help students to develop an awareness of the force with which Britain built and held on to its colonies and the extent of resistance that the colonized people mounted against their foreign rulers.

2   To encourage students to analyse some of the reasons for the differ-
    ent interpretations of history.

Students' Work Sheet

Historical interpretations of the Indian War of Independence

Exercise 1

India's first national war against the British lasted from May 1857 to October
1858. This war spread through a vast area of India (the size of France, Austria and Prussia together) that had a population of 45 million. For over a year
the Indian people put up a remarkable resistance and Britain almost lost its
'jewel'.

A study of the interpretations of this war is interesting. The British
viewed the uprising as a 'mutiny' — which means the refusal of people under
discipline to accept orders. The Indian men in the British army were seen by
the British to rebel simply because they were being forced to grease the
cartridges of their guns with the fat of pigs and cows. Such practices were
against the faith of the Muslims who religiously abstained from eating pork
and against the faith of the Hindus who did not eat beef for religious reasons.
Indeed, the use of lard for the purposes of greasing cartridges was a matter
of concern for the Indian men in the British army. However, the British in
their interpretation of this war did not acknowledge the major grievances of
the Indian people, which were the results of British rule in India — massive
unemployment, landlessness and famines. Furthermore, the Indian men in
the British army were compelled consistently to go abroad to fight Britain's
wars. The Indian men in the British army who rebelled against their masters did
so, not simply because of the lard that they were being forced to use for greasing their cartridges, but because they could no longer tolerate the position of
their people and themselves in India under British rule. By calling this war
a mutiny, the British attempted to mask the widespread discontent of the
Indian people in the whole of India, and focused only on the British army.

It was in the interest of the British to record this war as the Indian
Mutiny, the cause of which was considered to be a religious grievance against
the use of lard for greasing rifle cartridges. Indian historians have named this
war the 'National War of Independence' and have argued that the causes of
this war were numerous:

> The British, under the East India Company's rule, disrupted the whole
> economic order of India, they turned the traditional land system
> topsy-turvy, they smashed the trades and manufacturers of the land
> and disrupted the relationship between these two sectors of the
> Indian economy, systematically drained the wealth of our country
> to their own, and destroyed the very springs of production of our

economy. Every class of Indian society suffered at this new spoliator hands. The landlords were dispossessed and the peasants rendered paupers, the merchant bourgeoisie of India liquidated as an independent class and the artisans and craftsmen deprived of their productive professions. Such unprecedented destruction of a whole economic order and of every class within it could not but produce a great social upheaval and that was the national uprising of 1857. The all-destructive British policy produced a broad popular rebellion against its rule. (Embree, 1987, p. 117)

Questions: What were the causes of the 1857–1858 war in India?
Why did the British call this war the 'mutiny'?
Why did the Indian people call this war 'The National War of Independence'?

Exercise 2

Britain retaliated ruthlessly and won this war by butchering thousands of Indians. Sir John Kaye in *History of the Sepoy War in India* described this succinctly. He wrote:

> our military officers hunting down criminals of all kinds, and hanging them up with as little compunction as though they had been pariah dogs or jackals, or vermin of a baser kind.... Volunteer hanging parties went onto the districts, and amateur executioners were not wanting to the occasion. One gentleman boasted of the number he had finished off quite 'in an artistic manner', with mango trees as gibbets and elephants for drops, the victims of this wild justice being strung up as though for pastime, in 'the form of a figure eight'. (Kaye, J.W. 1864–76, pp. 170, 235–7)

There was much bloodshed, and many Indian and British people died. The Indian national uprising failed primarily because the British had better war weapons — the newly invented Enfield rifle and access to a good communication system — the telegraph. Nevertheless, the resistance of the Indian people was kept alive until finally India gained its independence on 14 August 1947.

Questions: Why did the Indian people lose this war?
Why did the British win this war?

Exercise 3

Group A
Prepare a talk on the position of the Indian people under British rule. Present the talk to the rest of the class.

Figure 14: Assault of Delhi
On 14 September 1857 the British force delivered their assault on Delhi for which preparations had been made by them for nearly three months. The sketch represents the fierce fighting of that day. The Indian troops fought with courage and did not yield an inch without desperate struggle. They, however, failed to keep the foreigners out of the imperial city. The English victory was secured at the cost of very heavy losses.

Group B
Prepare a talk on the reasons for the Indian War of Independence through the eyes of the Indian people. Present the talk to the rest of the class.

Group C
Prepare a talk on the reasons for the Indian War of Independence often being referred to as 'The Mutiny'. Present the talk to the rest of the class.

Activity: Write an essay on how the British people's attitude to the Indian War of Independence reflected the colonial relationship that Britain had with India.

Resource Books for Teachers

EMBREE, A.T. (1987) *India in 1857: The Revolt Against Foreign Rule*, Delhi, Chanakya Publications.

FRYER, P. (1988) *Black People in the British Empire: An Introduction,* London, Pluto Press.

KAYE, J.W. (1864–76) *A History of the Sepoy War in India: 1857–8*, London, W.H. Allen and Co.

SANDWELL DEPARTMENT OF EDUCATION (1987) *Britain and India: An Uncommon Journey*, (Units 1, 2 & 3) Sandwell, Education Development Centre.

Key Stage Four: Supplementary Unit B

One of the Supplementary Study Units in Key Stage Four is 'The Middle East, 1914 to 1967 (from the First World War to the Six Day Arab-Israeli War)'. This is a vast area of history and teachers may wish to include many historic events and struggles of this period. The following lesson plan is offered as part of this Supplementary Study Unit. A study of the founding of the State of Israel encompasses many of the complex forces at work between 1914 and 1967 in the Middle East. Numerous countries in the Middle East were engaged in anti-colonial struggles and the Western European nations were involved in realigning their power bases in this strategically important part of the world. The aims of this lesson plan are to offer students some information about the history of the Middle East between 1914 and 1967, and to encourage students to analyse the reasons behind the different interpretations of twentieth-century history of this part of the world.

Students' Work Sheet

Exercise 1: The Founding of the State of Israel

Towards the end of the nineteenth century anti-Semitism intensified, and Jewish people suffered increasingly from its effects. Jewish leaders in Eastern

Europe attempted to find a solution for the oppression of their sisters and brothers. In 1882, Leo Pinsker wrote a pamphlet entitled 'The Emancipation of the Jews'. In it he argued that Jews throughout the world had always been forced to work in finance and trade; as a result, they had lost the respect of the working population, whose involvement with the production process gave them stronger ties with the land. Pinsker proposed that that the Jews should take their destiny into their own hands, colonize the land and cultivate the earth. In 1884, he founded the Friends of Zion and shortly afterwards the first Zionists emigrated from Romania to Palestine (Pinsker, 1882 in Frangi, 1982, p. 29).

The first Jewish settlers in Palestine lived in harmony with the Arab population, but as anti-Semitism in Europe escalated during the First World War, European Zionism took on a different, more radical direction. The Zionists' search for a homeland became a priority as preparations to make Palestine into a Jewish State began. The Zionist leaders sought help from all the leading Western European nations and Britain was not alone in offering support.

The Balfour Declaration

His Majesty's Government [of Britain] views with favour the estab-lishment in Palestine a national home for the Jewish people, and will use their best endeavours to facilitate the achievement of this object. (Frangi, 1982, p. 42)

The Nazi's systematic destruction of Jewish people in Germany led to an even more determined effort by the Zionists to build a Jewish state. In 1919, Rosenblatt, a Jewish-American lawyer who was working towards developing support for the founding of the State of Israel stated:

Now that we have convinced the powerful governments of Great Britain, France and Italy and gained the support of the Pope and finally of the President of the United States, we feel that we have won our case in the eyes of the world and that it is completely futile to waste valuable energy trying to convert a negligible small oppo-sition.... (Rosenblatt, 1919, in Frangi, 1982, p. 43)

The State of Israel was founded on 15th May 1948.

Activity: Outline the factors that have contributed towards the formation of the state of Israel.

Exercise 2: The Oppression of Palestinians

With the support of the powerful nations in Western Europe, the Zionists colonized Palestine. Numerous strategies were employed by the Zionists to achieve their goal and terrorizing the inhabitants of Palestine was one of them:

> After 15 May 1948, the Israeli army attacked countless defenceless Arab villages, blew up houses and entire villages and indiscriminately killed men, women and children. The survivors were driven out of the villages. News of these appalling massacres spread like wildfire and those who did not believe the reports were likely to become the next victims.
>
> The Israelis' psychological warfare was based on shock tactics. Israeli radio was constantly calling on the Palestinians to flee 'to avoid a bloodbath'. Israeli army vehicles with loudspeakers drove through the streets of the towns and villages pointing out the escape routes. . . . But rumours and radio reports were not the only reasons for panic and headlong flight. The Israeli army deliberately and systematically destroyed villages and drove out their inhabitants. (Frangi, 1982, p. 89)

Activity: Outline some of the methods used for the purpose of founding the state of Israel.

Exercise 3: The Palestinians leave their homeland

From spring 1948 to spring 1949, streams of refugees left the country, with the Israeli army behind them and an uncertain future before them. Families would often walk on at night and hide from Israeli attacks by day. (Frangi, 1982, p. 91)

The Palestinians had seen their villages destroyed, they had been forced to flee with nothing but what they could carry. Often enough this meant only their children. Yet they took with them something else as a token of their determination to return: the keys to the doors of their houses. These keys can still be seen hanging above the doors of small houses in refugee camps in Jordan, Syria and Lebanon, bearing silent but eloquent witness to the expulsion from and longing for Palestine. (Frangi, 1982, p. 91)

Right up to the present day, world opinion has taken little or no note of the atrocities Israel committed at that time. It would not and could not believe that the Jews, who had the whole-hearted sympathy of the entire world after their dreadful experiences under Nazism, could perpetrate such cruelties on another people. The Israelis themselves sowed the seeds of armed resistance in the hearts of the Palestinians at this time. Many acts by the Palestinians which world opinion would

Figure 15: A raid by the army
A scene from daily life in the camps where the Palestinians live. Drawn by a Palestinian child.

later condemn as terrorism can be better understood in the light of this historical background. (Frangi, 1982, p. 90)

Project:
(Work in groups of six)

The above are extracts taken from the book, *The PLO and Palestine*, 1982, London, Zed Books written by Abdallah Frangi, a representative of the Palestinian Liberation Organization which aims to work towards gaining human rights and self determination for the Palestinians in Israel.

1 Write to the Head Office of the Palestinian Liberation Organisation, 4 Clareville Grove, London, SW7 5AR for further information on the position of the Palestinian people in Israel between the period 1948 to 1964.
2 For the Israeli perspective on the position of the Palestinian people in Israel between 1948 and 1964, write for information to the Israeli Embassy at 2, Palace Green, London, W8 4QB.

Using the information collected from the above two organizations, prepare two exhibitions:

1 portraying the position of the Palestinians in Israel between 1948 and 1964 from the Palestinian perspective,
2 portraying the position of the Palestinians in Israel between 1948 and 1964 from the Israeli perspective.

Resource Books for Teachers

FRANGI, A. (1982) *The PLO and Palestine*, London, Zed Books.
GRESH, A. and VIDAL, D. (1988) *The Middle East: War Without End?* London, Lawrence and Wishart.
SAMARA, A. (1989) *Palestine: Profile of an Occupation*, London, Zed Books.

Assessment

The above outlines for lesson plans attempted to offer teachers some suggestions as to how an anti-racist thread could be woven into the teaching of history. The lesson plans are designed to meet the requirements of the Attainment Targets specified by the National History Curriculum. Below are some suggestions for assessing students' progress after they have worked through the study programmes outlined in this chapter. The assessment format follows the guidelines outlined by the National Curriculum and include,

Attainment Target 1: Knowledge and Understanding of history,
Attainment Target 2: Interpretations of history,
Attainment Target 3: The use of historical sources.

Attainment Target 1: Knowledge and understanding of history

The development of the ability to describe and explain historical change and cause, and analyse different features of historical situations.

Level	Statements of Attainment	Examples
	Demonstrating their knowledge of the historical content of the programmes of study, pupils should be able to:	
1	a) place in sequence events in a story about the past.	Talk about the creation of apartheid in South Africa

Level	Statements of Attainment	Examples
		and the oppression and the resistance of South African people.
	b) give reasons for their own actions	
2	a) place familiar objects in chronological order.	Make a family tree using family photographs or other family belongings.
	b) suggest reasons why people in the past acted as they did.	Explain why many white people did not treat black people as equals when black people came to work in Britain after the Second World War.
	c) identify differences between past and present times.	Discuss the differences in how black people were treated in Britain during the period of the slave trade and today.
3	a) describe changes over a period of time.	Draw a map illustrating the rise and fall of the ancient civilizations of the world.
	b) give a reason for an historical event or development	Explain why many scholars from Ancient Greece went to study in Egypt.
	c) Identify differences between times in the past.	Talk about the differences between the portrayal of African people in the paintings of the Egyptian civilization and the paintings of eighteenth century Britain.
4	a) recognize that over time some things changed and others stayed the same.	Discuss how even when the Crusaders had stopped conquering new lands, the religious justifications that they developed continued during the period of colonial conquest.
	b) show an awareness that historical events usually	Outline the religious, economic, social and political

Level	Statements of Attainment	Examples
	have more than one cause and consequence.	aims of the Crusades and how these affected the people who had been conquered.
	c) describe different features of an historical period.	Arrange, label and display pictures and maps which illustrate aspects of life during the Crusades.
5	a) distinguish between different kinds of historical change.	Group some of the changes in Britain and in Africa under the headings of 'development' and 'under-development' during the period of the Atlantic slave trade.
	b) identify different types of cause and consequence.	Suggest some of the economic, political and social factors that contributed towards Britain's transition from being a leading slave trading nation to being the biggest Empire in the world.
	c) show how different features in an historical situation relate to each other.	Write an account of British colonialism in India linking the different aspects of social, economic and political development in Britain and the under-development of India.
6	a) show an understanding that change and progress are not the same.	Describe how Britain's transition from being a small isolated island to a world imperial power did not bring progress to the people of Britain's empire.
	b) recognize that causes and consequences can vary in importance.	Discuss in a group what importance to attach to Britain's technological development and to Britain's slave trade and slave plantation systems as factors which contributed towards Britain's industrial revolution.

Level	Statements of Attainment	Examples
	c) describe the different ideas and attitudes of people in an historical situation.	Give an account of the development of British racism during the era of the slave trade.
7	a) show an awareness that patterns of change can be complex.	Identify the various ways in which the British Empire affected the people of Britain and the people of Britain's colonies.
	b) show how the different causes of an historical event are connected.	When explaining changes in living standards during the nineteenth century Britain, identify links between colonialism and socio-economic development.
	c) show an awareness that different people's ideas and attitudes are often related to their circumstances.	Show how Britain's colonial gain from the people and the countries of black people led many British people to accept a racist view of the world.
8	a) explain the relative importance of several linked causes.	Assess the effects of mass landlessness and unemployment on Indian people's decision to wage a war against the British rulers of India in 1857.
	b) show an understanding of the diversity of people's ideas, attitudes and circumstances in complex historical situations.	Show how the British people's attitude to the Indian War of Independence reflected the imperial relationship that the British had with India.
9	a) show an understanding of how causes, motives and consequences may be related.	Present to the class an account of the causes of the formation of the state of Israel and examine the rise of anti-Semitism in Europe at the turn of the century and the imperial aims of the British and other European nations in the middle east after the Second

Level	Statements of Attainment	Examples
		World War as contributory factors.
	b) explain why individuals did not necessarily share the ideas and attitudes of the groups and societies to which they belonged.	Outline the development of a sectarian opposition to home rule in Northern Ireland.
10	a) show an understanding of the issues involved in describing, analysing and explaining complex historical situations.	Discuss the factors which contributed towards the independence struggles in the colonies of the British Empire after the First World War.

Attainment Target 2: Interpretations of history

The development of the ability to understand interpretations of history.

Level	Statements of Attainment	Examples
	Demonstrating their knowledge of the historical content in the programmes of study, pupils should be able to:	
1	understand that stories may be about real people or fictional characters.	Recognize the difference between a fictional story such as Robinson Crusoe and the historical story about Sir John Hawkins who transported the first groups of slaves from Africa to the Americas in 1562.
2	show an awareness that different stories about the past can give different versions of what happened.	Detect the differences in one white and one black adult's accounts of why black people have come to Britain.
3	distinguish between a fact and a point of view.	Recognize that the view of some 'historians' that Africa had no civilization of its own is a point of view and that one of the first civilizations to evolve on this earth was in Africa is a fact.

Level	Statements of Attainment	Examples
4	show an understanding that deficiencies in evidence may lead to different interpretations of the past.	Show how the lack of records of how many slaves were transported from Africa to the Americas has led to different estimations of how many people Africa lost to this trade in human beings.
5	recognize that interpretation of the past, including popular accounts, may differ from what is known to have happened.	Explain why, although slave rebellions rendered slavery uneconomic, many British people today believe that the slaves were liberated because a wave of humanitarianism hit the British people.
6	demonstrate how historical interpretations depend on the selection of sources.	Show how the records of Britain's technological development as an historical source can lead to a limited understanding of Britain's industrial revolution.
7	describe the strengths and weaknesses of different interpretations of an historical event or development.	Investigate the extent to which films about the British Raj give accurate or complete accounts of events in the history of British rule in India.
8	show how attitudes and circumstances can influence an individual's interpretation of historical events or developments.	Comment on how far an account of the Indian War of Independence is likely to have been influenced by the background and political views of the writer
9	explain why different groups or societies interpret and use history in different ways.	Show how and why there have been different views of the creation of the State of Israel.
10	show an understanding of the issues involved in trying to make history as objective as possible.	Discuss the issues involved in trying to give an objective account of the development of the British Empire.

Attainment Target 3: The use of historical sources

The development of pupils' ability to acquire evidence from historical sources, and form judgements about their reliability and value.

Level	Statements of Attainment	Examples
	Demonstrating their knowledge of the historical content in the programmes of study, pupils should be able to:	
1	communicate information acquired from an historical source.	Comment on old photographs of Africa.
2	recognize that historical sources can stimulate and help answer questions about the past.	Show how artefacts in a museum can illustrate the creativity of people in different parts of the world at different times in history.
3	make deductions from historical sources.	Make deductions about the building and technical skills of the ancient Egyptians from a picture of the pyramids taking note of the size and structure of the pyramids.
4	put together information drawn from different historical sources.	Use information from old maps to describe the routes that the British Crusaders took during the medieval period.
5	comment on the usefulness of an historical source by reference to its content, as evidence for a particular enquiry.	Talk about how information gained from a hymn can be used to reconstruct some of the ideas of the people in nineteenth century Britain.
6	compare the usefulness of different historical sources as evidence for a particular enquiry.	Comment on the artistic impressions of black people in eighteenth century Britain.
7	make judgments about the reliability and value of historical sources by reference to the circumstances in which they were produced.	Discuss the reliability of the material produced by the British scientists in their efforts to suggest that the white people are of a superior race.

Level	Statements of Attainment	Examples
8	show how a source which is unreliable can nevertheless be useful.	Comment on the extent to which the work of the literary authors of nineteenth century Britain can be useful for understanding some of the ideas of the British people about their empire.
9	show an understanding that a source can be more or less valuable depending on the questions asked of it.	Analyse the material produced by the Israeli embassy regarding the position of the Palestinian people in the State of Israel.
10	explain the problematic nature of historical evidence, showing an awareness that judgments based on historical sources may well be provisional.	Explain how the limited recordings of the destructive impact of British imperialism in this world can make it difficult to form a complete picture of what took place during the British colonial era.

Conclusion

An imaginative adaptation of the National History Curriculum could be an opportunity to challenge the British state's plans to teach the next generation a limited history which does not threaten the unequal race, class and gender relations in our society. This chapter aimed to offer teachers some practical suggestions as to how they could offer their students some insight into the historical forces of oppression and liberation.

Conclusion

I do not write about the benevolent, enlightening mission of the British Empire although some people would feel more at ease with such a perspective. I write about how oppressive colonialism was for the people of the British Empire. In doing so, I expose the violence of colonialism. Such a historical account is seen by some as a strongly worded diatribe and for others, it is a factual account of the experiences of their ancestors. What should history teachers teach their students about the history of Great Britain?

While it is important not to lose sight of a country's heritage, it is also necessary to examine exactly how this was achieved. One of Britain's greatest achievements is often seen as the industrial revolution. Indeed this revolution did have something to do with the creativity of the inventors of machines that made mass production possible. However, the industrial revolution also had something to do with the enormous accumulation of capital that made it possible for Britain to transform its economic base from a feudal one to an industrial one. Much of this wealth was accumulated from the profits made by exploiting the labour of the British working-class children, women and men, as well the profits made by selling millions of Africans as slaves. Britain's Empire also played a significant role in sustaining the industrial revolution, for the colonies were cheap sources of raw materials and ready markets for the finished products.

The mighty position that Great Britain held in the world in the past would not have been possible without its massive empire. What should history students learn about the creation of the British Empire? Britain did not achieve its colonies through peaceful means and the aim of the empire was not to help poor, backward people. Before the days of the National Curriculum, when teachers attempted to grasp the thorny nettle of British imperialism and teach their students about colonial oppression and the history of racism, they were often accused of being 'inflammatory', and of using teaching materials that lacked 'balance', were 'biased' and contained 'discrepancies'.

In this book I have argued that the National History Curriculum attempts to teach students a limited history, a history that does not threaten the

British social order with its unequal race, gender and class relations. However, if the aim of history is to make sense of the past in order to understand the present and to respond to the future constructively, then history lessons should not be based primarily on the selected glories of the past. Fortunately, at present, the British State's National Curriculum is a broad outline of subject areas and teachers have the freedom to use teaching materials of their own choice. Thus teachers still have some possibilities of teaching their students a critical history of Britain.

Chapters 4 and 5 illustrated how teachers can liberate the National History Curriculum from the clutches of the British State and offer their students not only the history of racism but also the history of sexism and class oppression. In this way, the history of one oppressed group is not compartmentalized but is situated within the political economy of domination. The aim of liberating the National History Curriculum is not to be divisive but to seek a unity for the future by understanding and accepting the positive and the negative of our collective past. The positive elements of British history include the struggles for justice and the resistance of the people of the British Empire and Britain's working-class women and men and other minorities. The negative elements of British history include Britain's institutionalization of oppressive structures for the purpose of becoming rich.

A creative adaptation of the National Curriculum would offer students some insight into the dialectical nature of historical development and they would know that history is not simply a study of isolated, unrelated incidents and glories of the past. Students would also learn that history is a critical exploration of the historical social, economic and political forces that have impacted upon groups of people in the past and continue to do so today. This would make it possible for students not to blame the oppressed by arguing that social inequalities exist because of the biological make-up of some groups of people or because of the lifestyles of some people or even because of some divine force.

The National History Curriculum skims over the history of Britain's political economy of domination but if teachers could somehow manage to include the teaching of such a history, they would equip their students in a small way to understand and challenge oppression and inequalities in the society in which they live. What would be the consequences if history teachers choose to teach their students only what the British state dictates?

Key Stage 3 Core Study Unit 3
The making of the United Kingdom:
Crowns, Parliaments and peoples
1500 to 1750

Pupils should be taught about the major political, social and religious changes which shaped the history of Britain during this period. The main focus should be on two themes: the political unification of Britain, and the changing relationships between Crown, Parliament and people.

Pupils should be taught about:

the political unification of Britain	• the formation of the United Kingdom, including the Acts of Union of 1536 and 1543 (Wales) and the Treaty of 1707 (Scotland), and the changing relationship between England and Ireland
the power of the monarchy and its relationship with Parliament and people	• the functions and importance of the Crown the changing relationships of Crown, Parliament and people in the era of the Civil War and Interregnum (1639 to 1660) and Glorious Revolution (1688)
changes in ideas and the arts	• the impact on the arts and architecture of political and religious change the scientific revolution of the seventeenth century

the diversity of British Society	• social classes in early modern Britain
	regional differences in wealth, lifestyle, religion and culture
	religious differences and relations between Roman Catholics, Anglicans and Nonconformists

(DES, 1991, p. 41).

Appendix 2

Key Stage 3
Supplementary Study Units

Pupils should be taught **three** study units, one from each of categories A, B, and C. Each unit should make demands comparable to those of a core study unit, in historical knowledge, understanding and skills.

A) **A unit which extends the study of the core British study units for this key stage.** This unit should:

* relate to the history of the British Isles before 1920;
* involve **either** a study in depth **or** the study of a theme over a long period of time.

Examples

> *Castles and cathedrals 1066 to 1500*
>
> *Relations between England and Scotland from the Norman conquest to the Treaty of Union*
>
> *Culture and society in Ireland from early times to the beginning of the twentieth century*
>
> *Britain and the American Revolution*
>
> *The impact of the Industrial Revolution on a local area*
>
> *The British Empire and its impact in the last quarter of the nineteenth century*
>
> *Britain and the Great War 1914 to 1918*

(DES, 1991, p. 47)

References

ACKER, A. (1988) *Honduras: The Making of a Banana Republic*, Toronto, Between the Lines.

ADELMAN, P. (1982) *Victorian Radicalism: The Middle-Class Experience 1830–1914*, Harlow, Longman.

AFFOR (1983) *A Handbook for Teachers in the Multicultural Society: Issues and Resources*, Birmingham, Affor.

AKBAR, M.J. (1985) *India: The Siege Within, Challenges to a Nation's Unity*, Harmondsworth, Penguin.

ALEXANDER, Z. and DEWJEE, A. (1981) *Roots in Britain: Black and Asian Citizens from Elizabeth I to Elizabeth II*, London, Brent Library Service.

ALLEN, I. (1987) *Education in Sex and Personal Relationships*, Policy Studies Unit.

ALI, T. (1983) *Can Pakistan Survive? The Death of a State*, Harmondsworth, Penguin.

ALI, T. (1987) *An Autobiography of the Sixties Street Fighting Years*, London, W. Collins and Sons.

ALLCHIN, B. and ALLCHIN, R. (1982) *The Rise of Civilization in India and Pakistan*, London, Cambridge University Press.

ALTHUSSER, L. (1971) 'Ideology and ideological state apparatuses', in COSIN, B.R. (Ed) (1972) *Education: Structure and Society*, London, Penguin.

AMAMOO, J.G. (1988) *The Ghanaian Revolution*, London, Jafint Co.

AMIN, S., CHITALA, D. and MANDAZA, I. (Eds) (1987) *SADCC: Prospects for Disengagement and Development in Southern Africa*, London, Zed Books.

ANGELOU, M. (1984) *Feminist Review No. 17: Many Voices, One Chant. Black Feminist Perspectives*, London, The Feminist Review Collective.

ARORA, R. and DUNCAN, C. (Eds) (1986) *Multicultural Education Towards Good Practice*, London, Routledge and Kegan Paul.

BALDWIN, J. (1962) *The Fire Next Time*, New York, Dial Press.

BARRACLOUGH, S.L. and SCOTT, M.F. (1987) *The Rich Have Already Eaten Roots of Catastrophe in Central America*, Amsterdam, Transnational Institute.

BARRETT, M. and PHILLIPS, A. (Eds) (1992) *Destabilizing Theory: Contemporary Feminist Debates*, Cambridge, Polity Press.

BECK, J., JENKS, C., KEDDIE, N. and YOUNG, M.F.D. (Eds) (1976) *Worlds Apart: Readings for a Sociology of Education*, London, Collier-Macmillan.

BECKETT, J.C. (1966) *The Making of Modern Ireland 1603–1923*, London, Faber.

BECKFORD, G. and WITTER, M. (1980) *Small Garden, Bitter Weed — Struggle and Change in Jamaica*, London, Zed Press.

BENDIX, R. and LIPSET, S.M. (Eds) (1967) *Class, Status, and Power*, London, Routledge and Kegan Paul.

BERNAL, M. (1987) *Black Athena: The Afroasiatic Roots of Classical Civilisation*, **1**, London, Free Association Books.

BHAVNANI, K. and COULSON, M. 'Transforming Socialist-Feminism: The Challenge of Racism' No. 23, pp. 81–92, in Feminist Review, (1986) Socialist Feminism Out of the Blue, London, Feminist Review Collective.

Bible, Revised Standard Version, 1952 Edition, London, Collins.

BIKO, S. (1978) *I Write What I Like*, London, Heinemann.

BILTON, T., BENNETT, K., JONES, P., STANWORTH, M., SHEARD, K. and WEBSTER, A. (1981) *Introducing Sociology*, London, Macmillan.

BIRD, E. *et al.* (The Bristol Women's Studied Group) (1979) *The Sky, An Introduction to Women's Studies*, London, Virago.

BLYTH, J. (1988) *History 5 to 9*, London, Hodder and Stoughton.

BOHM, R. (1982) *Notes on India*, Boston, South End Press.

BOLTON, D. (1985) *Nationalism: A Road to Socialism? The Case of Tanzania*, London, Zed Press.

BOOTH, C. (1887) 'The inhabitants of Tower Hamlets (School Board Division). Their conditions and occupation', *The Journal of the Royal Statistical Society*, London.

BOSERUP, E. (1970) *Women's Role in Economic Development*, USA, St. Martin's Press.

BRAIDOTTI, R. (1991) *Patterns of Dissonance. A Study of Women and Contemporary Philosophy*, Cambridge, Polity Press (Translated by Elizabeth Guild).

BRANDT, G.L. (1986) *The Realisation of Anti-racist Teaching*, London, Falmer Press.

BRITAIN, V. and MINTY, A.S. (1988) *Children of Resistance on Children, Repression and the Law in Apartheid South Africa*, London, Kliptown Books.

BRYAN, B., DADZIE, S. and SCAFE, S. (1985) *The Heart of the Race*, London, Virago.

BUDIARDJO, C., LIONG, L.S. (1983) *West Papua: The Obliteration of a People*, Surrey, TAPOL.

BURGER, J. (1987) *Report from the Frontier: The State of the World's Indigenous Peoples*, London, Zed Press.

BUSH, M. (Ed) (1991) *Social Orders and Social Classes in Europe since 1500: Studies in Social Stratification*, Harlow, Longman.

CAPLAN, A.L., ENGELHARDT, H.T. and McCARTNEY, J.J. (Eds) (1981) *Concepts of Health and Disease, Interdisciplinary Perspectives*, USA, Addison-Wesley.

CARBY, H.V. (1982) 'Schooling in Babylon', in CENTRE FOR CONTEMPORARY CULTURAL STUDIES, *The Empire Strikes Back. Race and Racism in 70s Britain*, London, Hutchinson and Co. Ltd.

CARTER, A. (1966) *Race Relations in Britain*, London, Lawrence and Wishart.

CHATTERJEE, P. (1986) *Nationalist Thought and the Colonial World — A Derivative Discourse*, London, Zed Books.

CHELES, L., FERGUSON, R. and VAUGHAN, M. (Eds) (1991) *Neo-Facism in Europe*, Harlow, Longman.

CHIRIMUUTA, R.C. and CHIRIMUUTA, R.J. (1987) *Aids, Africa and Racism*, Bretby, Chirimuuta.

CLARK, D. (Ed) (1991) *Marriage, Domestic Life and Social Change, Writings for Jacqueline Burgoyne 1944–88*, London, Routledge.

COARD, B. (1971) *How the West Indian Child is made Educationally Subnormal in the British School System*, London, New Beacon Books.

COLTHAN, J.B. and FINES, J.F. (1971) *Educational Objectives for the Study of History: A Suggested Framework*, London, The Historical Association.

COMMISSION FOR RACIAL EQUALITY (1988) *Learning in Terror: A Survey of Racial Harrassment in Schools and Colleges*, London, C.R.E.

COMMONWEALTH IMMIGRANTS ADVISORY COUNCIL (CIAC) (1964) *Second Report (Cmnd 2266)*, London, HMSO.

COMMONWEALTH IMMIGRANTS ADVISORY COUNCIL (CIAC) (1964) *Third Report (Cmnd 2458)*, London, HMSO.

CORFIELD, P.J. (Ed) (1991) *Language, History and Class*, Oxford, Blackwell.

COTTERELL, A. (1980) *The Penguin Encyclopaedia of Ancient Civilisations*, Harmondsworth, Penguin.

COX, D. (1970) *Caste, Class and Race*, New York, Monthly Review Press (first published in 1948).

CROLL, E. (1983) *Chinese Women since Mao*, London, Zed Press.

CUNNINGHAM, H. (1991) *The Children of the Poor: Representations of Childhood since the Seventeenth Century*, Oxford, Blackwell.

CURTIS, L. (1984) *Nothing But the Same Old Story — The roots of Anti-Irish Racism*, London, Information on Ireland.

DABYDEEN, D. (1987) *Hogarth's Blacks: Images of Blacks in Eighteenth Century English Art*, Manchester, Manchester University Press.

DAVID, M. (1992) *Parents, Gender and Education Reform*, Cambridge, Polity Press.

DAVIDSON, B. (1983) *Modern Africa*, Harlow, Longman.

DAVIDSON, B. (1989) *Modern Africa*, Harlow, Longman.

DAVIES, M. (Ed) (1983) *Third World Second Sex, Women's Struggles and National Liberation, Third World Women Speak Out*, London, Zed Books.

DAVIES, R., O'MEARA, D. and DLAMINI, S. (1984) *The Struggle for South*

Africa: A Reference Guide to Movements, Organisations and Institutions, London, Zed Press.

DAVIS, A. (1982) *Women, Race and Class,* London, Women's Press.

DAVIS, K. and MOORE, W.E. (1945) 'Some principles of stratification', *American Sociological Review,* **10**, pp. 242–9.

DE BAROID, C. (1989) *Ballymurphy and the Irish War,* Baile Atha Cliath 4, Aisling Publishers.

DELPHY, C. and LEONARD, D. (1992) *Familiar Inequalities,* Cambridge, Polity Press.

DEPARTMENT OF EDUCATION AND SCIENCE (DES) (1965) *The Education of Immigrants, Circular 7/65,* London, HMSO.

DEPARTMENT OF EDUCATION AND SCIENCE (DES) (1975) 'Curriculum differences for boys and girls', *Education Survey 21,* London, HMSO.

DEPARTMENT OF EDUCATION AND SCIENCE (DES) (1981) 'West Indian children in British schools', *A Report of the Committee of Enquiry into the Education of Children from Ethnic Minority Groups (The Rampton Report),* London, HMSO.

DEPARTMENT OF EDUCATION AND SCIENCE (DES) (1985) *Education for All (The Swann Report), Cmnd 9453,* London, HMSO.

DEPARTMENT OF EDUCATION AND SCIENCE (DES) (1990) *National Curriculum History Working Group Final Report,* London, HMSO.

DEPARTMENT OF EDUCATION AND SCIENCE (DES) (1991) *History in the National Curriculum (England and Wales),* London, HMSO.

DICKINSON, A.K. and LEE, P.J. (1978) *History Teaching and Historical Understanding,* London, Heinemann.

DICKINSON, P. (1982) 'Facts and figures: Some myths', in TIERNEY, J. *Race Migration and Schooling,* Eastbourne, Holt, Rinehart and Winson.

DOUGLAS, M. (1970) *Natural Symbols,* London, Barrie and Jenkins.

DOYAL, L. (1983) *The Political Economy of Health,* London, Pluto Press.

DUBOIS, W.E.B. (1946) *The World and Africa,* New York, International Publishers Co.

DUMMET, A. and MARTIN, I. (1982) *British Nationality,* London, National Council for Civil Liberties.

DUNBAR ORTIZ, R. (1984) *Indians of the Americas: Human Rights and Self-determination,* London, Zed Press.

DUNKERLEY, J. (1984) *Rebellion in the Veins: Political Struggle in Bolivia 1952–1982,* London, VERSO.

DUTT, R.P. (1940) *India Today,* London, Victor Gollancz.

DYER, A.M. (1982) *History in a Multi-Cultural Society,* London, The Historical Association.

EDHOLM, F. (Ed) (1982) *Education Repression Chile,* London, World University Service.

EDWARDS, M. (1963) *The Last Years of British India,* Cleveland, World Publishing Co.

EMBREE, A.T. (1987) *India in 1857: The Revolt Against Foreign Rule*, Delhi, Chanakya Publications.

EVAN, B. and WAITES, B. (1981) *IQ and Mental Testing, An Unnatural Science and its Social History*, London, Macmillan Press.

EYSENCK, H.J. (1971) *Race, Intelligence and Education*, London, Temple Smith.

FANON, F. (1963) *The Wretched of the Earth*, Harmondsworth, Penguin.

FANON, F. (1952) *Black Skins White Masks*, London, Pluto Press.

FERGUSON, G.O. (1916) *The Psychology of the Negro: An Experimental Study*, New York, The Science Press.

FIRESTONE, S. (1972) *The Dialectic of Sex*, London, Paladin.

FONT, M. (1990) *Coffee, Contention, and Change in The Making of Modern Brazil*, Oxford, Blackwell.

FORDE, F., HALL, L. and McLEAN, V. (1989) *Black Makers of History: Not just Singin' and Dancin'*, London, The Bookplace.

FRANGI, A. (1982) *The PLO and Palestine*, London, Zed Books.

FRANK, A.G. (1967) *Capitalism and Underdevelopment in Latin America: Historical Studies of Chile and Brazil*, New York, Monthly Review Press.

FRANK, A.G. (1969) *Latin America: Underdevelopment or Revolution. Essays on the Development of Underdevelopment and the Immediate Enemy*, New York, Monthly Review Press.

FREIRE, P. (1972) *Cultural Action for Freedom*, Harmondsworth, Penguin.

FREIRE, P. (1972) *Pedagogy of the Oppressed*, Harmondsworth, Penguin.

FREIRE, P. (1978) *Pedagogy in Process: The Letters to Guinea-Bissau*, New York, Seabury Press.

FRIEDMAN, N.L. (1976) 'Cultural deprivation: A Commentary on the sociology of knowledge', in BECK, J., JENKS, C., KEDDIE, N. and YOUNG, M.F.D. (Eds) *Worlds Apart: Readings for a Sociology of Education*, London, Collier-Macmillan.

FRYER, P. (1984) *Staying Power: The History of Black People in Britain*, London, Pluto Press.

FRYER, P. (1988) *Black People in the British Empire: An Introduction*, London, Pluto Press.

GADANT, M. (Ed) (1986) *Women of the Mediterranean*, London, Zed Press.

GARDEZI, H. and RASHID, J. (1983) *Pakistan — The Roots of Dictatorship: The Political Economy of a Praetorian State*, London, Zed Press.

GARRIDO, G.T. (1985) *A Popular History of Two Revolutions: Guatemala and Nicaragua*, San Francisco, Synthesis Publications.

GATENS, M. (1991) *Feminism and Philosophy: Perspectives on Difference and Equality*, Cambridge, Polity Press.

GENOVESE, E. (1974) *Roll Jordan Roll: The World the Slaves Made*, New York, Pantheon.

GILROY, P. (1987) *There Ain't No Black in the Union Jack*, London, Hutchinson.

GOUGH, K. and SHARMA, H.P. (1973) *Imperialism and Revolution in South Asia*, New York, Monthly Review Press.

GRAML, H. (1992) *Anti-Semitism and its Origins in the Third Reich*, Oxford, Blackwell [Translated by Timothy Kirk].

GRESH, A. and VIDAL, D. (1988) *The Middle East: War Without End?*, London, Lawrence and Wishart.

GRIFFITHS, J. and GRIFFITHS, P. (1979) *Cuba: The Second Decade*, London, Writers and Readers.

GRIMAL, N. (1992) *A History of Ancient Egypt*, Oxford, Blackwell (Translated by Ian Shaw).

GUNDARA, J. (1982) 'Approaches to multicultural education', in TIERNEY, J. *Race, Colonialism and Migration*, Eastbourne, Holt, Rinehart and Winston.

GUTMAN, H. (1977) *The Black Family in Slavery and Freedom*, New York, Random House.

HALL, C. (1992) *White, Male and Middle Class: Exploration of Feminism and History*, Cambridge, Polity Press.

HALLO, W.W. and SIMPSON, W.K. (1971) *The Ancient Near East: A History*, London, Harcourt Brace Jovanovich.

HARALAMBOS, M. (1980) *Sociology, Themes and Perspectives*, Slouth, University Tutorial Press.

HARGREAVES, J.D. (1988) *Decolonization in Africa*, Harlow, Longman.

HARRIS, S. (1990) *Lesbian and Gay Issues in the English Classroom*, London, Open University Press.

HART, R. (1985) *Slaves Who Abolished Slavery: Blacks in Rebellion*, **2**, Jamaica, Institute of Social and Economic Research.

HEEHS, P. (1991) *India's Freedom Struggle 1857–1947: A Short History*, Oxford, Oxford University Press.

HENSMAN, C.P. (1971) *Rich against Poor*, Harmondsworth, Penguin.

HERBSTEIN, D. and EVENSON, J. (1989) *The Devils are Among Us: The War for Namibia*, London, Zed Press.

HESSARI, R. and HILL, D. (1989) *Practical Ideas for Multi-Cultural Learning and Teaching in the Primary Classroom*, London, Routledge.

HILL, C. (1972) *The World Turned Upside Down: Radical Ideas During the English Revolution*, Harmondsworth, Penguin.

HIRO, D. (1971) *Black British, White British*, London, Monthly Review Press.

HOBSBAWN, E.J. (1968) *Industry and Empire*, London, Penguin.

HOME OFFICE (1981) *Report of the Enquiry by the Right Hon. The Lord Scarman, OBE, (The Brixton Disorders 10–12 April, 1981) Cmnd. 8427*, London, HMSO.

HOOKS, B. (1982) *Aint I a Woman, Black Women and Feminism*, London, Pluto.

HOOKS, B. (1989) *Talking Back, Thinking Feminist, Thinking Black*, London, Sheba Feminist.

HOOKS, B. (1992) *Black Looks, Race and Representation*, London, Turnaround.

HOSKINS, W.G. (1976) *The Age of Plunder: The England of Henry VIII, 1500–1547*, Harlow, Longman.

HOULBROOKE, R.A. (1984) *The English Family 1450–1700*, Harlow, Longman.

HUMPHRIES, S. (1984) *The Handbook of Oral History: Recording Life Stories*, London, Inter-Action Inprints.

HUMPHRY, D. and JOHN, G. (1972) *Policy Power and Black People*, London, Panther Books Ltd.

HUNT, J. (1863) *On the Negro's Place in Nature*, London, Trubner and Co.

HYMAN, H.H. (1967) 'The value systems of different classes', in BENDIX, R. and LIPSET, S.M. (Eds), *Class, Status and Power*, London, Routledge and Kegan Paul.

INSTITUTE OF RACE RELATIONS (1982) Book One: *Roots of Racism*, London, Institute of Race Relations.

INSTITUTE OF RACE RELATIONS (1982) Book Two: *Patterns of Racism*, London, Institute of Race Relations.

INSTITUTE OF RACE RELATIONS (1985) Book Three: *How Racism Came to Britain*, London, Institute of Race Relations.

JAMES, A. and JEFFCOATE, R. (Eds) (1981) *The School in the Multicultural Society*, London, Harper and Row.

JEFFCOATE, R. (1984) *Ethnic Minorities and Education*, London, Harper and Row.

JEFFS, T. and SMITH, M. (Eds) (1990) *Young People, Inequality and Youth Work*, London, Macmillan.

JELIN, E. (Ed) (1990) *Women and Social Change in Latin America*, London, Zed Press.

JENSEN, A.R. (1973) *Educational Differences*, London, Methuen.

JENSEN, A.R. (1969) 'How much can we boost IQ and scholastic achievement?', in *Harvard Educational Review*, **39**.

JENSEN, A.R. (1972) *Education and Genetics*, London, Methuen.

JOHNSON, H. and BERNSTEIN, H. (1982) *Third World Lives of Struggle*, London, Heinemann.

JOSHI, B.R. (Ed) (1986) *Untouchable! Voices of the Dalit Liberation Movement*, London, Zed Books.

KAMIN, L. (1977) (first published 1974) *The Science and Politics of IQ*, Harmondsworth, Penguin.

KAYE, J.W. (1864–76) *A History of the Sepoy War in India: 1857–8*, London, W.H. Allen and Co.

KENT BAGULEY, P. (1988) 'One too many' *Youth and Policy*, **24**, Spring 1988.

KIPLING, R. (1977) *Selected Verses*, Harmondsworth, Penguin.

LAWRENCE, E. (1982) 'Just plain common sense: the "roots" of racism', in *Centre for Contemporary Studies* (op. cit.).

LAWRENCE, W. (1819) *Lecture on Physiology, Zoology and the Natural History of Man*, London, Callow.

LEFEBVRE, H. (1966) *The Sociology of Marx*, Harmondsworth, Penguin.

LEITE DA SILVA DIAS, M.O. (1992) *Power and Everyday Life: The Lives of Working Women in Nineteenth-Century Sao Paolo*, Cambridge, Polity Press.

References

LEKACHMAN, R. and VAN LOON, B. (1981) *Capitalism for Beginners*, London, Writers and Readers Publishing Cooperative Ltd.

LEMMA, A. and PENTTI, M. (Eds) (1990) *Africa Beyond Famine*, London, Cassell.

LEVACK, B.P. (1987) *The Witch-Hunt in Early Modern Europe*, Harlow, Longman.

LEWIS, R. (1988) *Anti-Racism — A Mania Exposed*, London, Quartet.

LOCKHART, J. and SCHWARTZ, S.B. (1983) *Early Latin America*, London, Cambridge University Press.

LOW, D.A. (1973) *Lion Rampant — Studies in British Imperialism*, London, Class University.

LOWN, J. (1990) *Women and Industrialization: Gender and Work in Nineteenth-Century England*, Cambridge, Polity Press.

LYONS, F.S.L. (1971) *Ireland Since the Famine*, London, Fontana.

LYONS, F.S.L. (1979) *Culture and Anarchy in Ireland 1890–1939*, Oxford, Oxford University Press.

MACDONALD, J.J. (1981) *The Theory and Practice of Integrated Rural Development*, Manchester, Manchester University Monographs.

MAJUMDAR, R.C., DATTA, K. and RAYCHAUDHURI, H.C. (1946) *An Advanced History of India*, London, Macmillan.

MATSUI, Y. (1989) *Women's Asia*, London, Zed Press.

MAYS, P. (1974) *Why Teach History?* London, University of London Press.

McCLINTOCK, M. (1985) *The American Connection: State Terror and Popular Resistance in Guatemala*, **2**, London, Zed Press.

McCLINTOCK, M. (1985) *The American Connection: State Terror and Popular Resistance in El Salvador*, London, Zed Press.

McDOWELL, L. and PRINGLE, R. (Eds) (1992) *Defining Women: Social Institutions and Gender Divisions*, Cambridge, Polity Press.

MEMMI, A. (1965) *Colonizer Colonized*, New York, The Orion Press.

MILNE, K. (1979) *New Approaches to the Teaching of Irish History*, London, The Historical Association, No. 43.

MILNER, D. (1975) *Children and Race*, Harmondsworth, Penguin.

MONK, W.H. (1875) *Hymns Ancient and Modern*, London, W. Clowes.

MUKHERJEE, R. (1974) *The Rise and Fall of the East India Company*, London, Monthly Review Press.

MULLARD, C. (1982) 'Multi-racial education in Britain: From assimilation to cultural pluralism', in TIERNEY, J. *Race, Colonialism and Migration*, Eastbourne, Holt, Rinehart and Winston.

MURPHY, L. and LIVINGSTONE, J. 'Racism and the limits of radical feminism', in *Race and Class*, **XXVI**, 4, London, Institute for Race Relations.

NASH, J. and SAFA, H. (Eds) (1985) *Women and Change in Latin America*, Massachusetts, Bergin and Garvey Publishers.

NATIONAL ASSOCIATION FOR MULTICULTURAL EDUCATION (1982) *Multiracial Education*, **10**, 2, London, N.A.M.E.

NATIONAL CURRICULUM COUNCIL (1990a) *National Curriculum Guidance No. 5 Health Education*, York, National Curriculum Council.

NATIONAL CURRICULUM COUNCIL (1990b) *History in the National Curriculum Consultation Report*, York, National Curriculum Council.

NATIONAL CURRICULUM COUNCIL (1991) *History Non-Statutory Guidance*, York, National Curriculum Council.

NATIONAL FOUNDATION FOR EDUCATIONAL RESEARCH (1966) *Coloured Immigrant Children: A Survey of Research, Studies and Literature on their Educational Problems and Potential in Britain*, London, NFER.

NAVARRO, V. (1986) *Crisis, Health and Medicine — A Social Critique*, London, Tavistock.

New Internationalist (1989) No. 200, October, pp. 6–8.

NKRUMAH, K. (1963) *Africa Must Unite*, London, Panaf Books.

NKRUMAH, K. (1965) *Neo-Colonialism: The Last Stage of Imperialism*, London, Panaf Books.

NYONG'O, P.A. (Ed) (1987) *Popular Struggles for Democracy in Africa*, London, Zed Books.

OHRI, A., MANNINGS, B., CURNO, P. (1982) *Community Work and Racism*, London, Routledge and Kegan Paul.

PARMAR, P. *Gender race and Class: Asian Women in Resistance*, in Contemporary Cultural Studies, (1982) The Empire Strikes Back, Race and Racism in 70s Britain, London, Hutchinson and Co.

PARSONS, T. (1961) 'The school class as a social system', in HALSEY, A.H. (Ed) (1977) *Power and Ideology in Education*, New York, Oxford University Press.

PEARCE, J. (1986) *Promised Land: Peasant Rebellion in Chalatenango El Salvador*, London, Latin American Bureau (Research and Action).

PHIMISTER, I. (1988) *An Economic and Social History of Zimbabwe 1890–1948: Capital Accumulation and Class Struggle*, Harlow, Longman.

PIMLOTT, B. (1991) *Trade Unions in British Politics: The First 250 Years*, Harlow Longman.

PLANT, R. (1987) *Sugar and Modern Slavery: A Tale of Two Countries*, London, Zed Press.

POLLARD, D. (1988) *Give and Take: The Losing Partnership in Aboriginal Poverty*, Sydney, Hale and Iremonger.

PORTER, B. (1984) *The Lion's Share: A short History of British Imperialism 1850–1970*, London, Longman.

POSTAN, M.M. (1972) *The Medieval Economy and Society*, Harmondsworth, Penguin Books.

PREBBLE, J. (1963) *The Highland Clearances*, Harmondsworth, Penguin.

PRYCE, K. (1979) *Endless Pressure*, Harmondsworth, Penguin.

QUNTA, C. (1987) *Women in Southern Africa*, London, A and B. Co. Ltd.

RANDELL, K. (1976) *Resources for the Teaching of History in Secondary Schools*, London, The Historical Association.

RANGER, T. (1985) *Peasant Consciousness and Guerrilla War in Zimbabwe*, London, J. Currey.

RAUF, A. (1983) 'Education and development', in GARDEZI, H. and RASHID, J.

REID, M. (1985) *Peru. Paths to Poverty*, London, Latin American Bureau Research and Action.

REYNOLDS, E. (1985) *Stand the Storm: A History of the Atlantic Slave Trade*, London, Allison and Busby.

ROBINSON, C. (1979) 'The emergence and limitations of European radicalism', in *Race and Class*, **XXI**, 2, London, Institute for Race Relations.

ROBINSON, M. (1991) *Family Transformation During Divorce and Remarriage: A Systemic Approach*, London, Routledge.

RODNEY, W. (1966) 'African slavery and other forms of social oppression of the Upper Guinea Coast in the context of the Atlantic Slave Trade', in *Journal of African History*, **VIII**, 3.

RODNEY, W. (1970) *West Africa and the Atlantic Slave Trade*, Lagos, Afrografika Publishers.

RODNEY, W. (1972) *How Europe Underdeveloped Africa*, London, Bogle-L'Ouverture Publications.

RULE, J. (1986) *The Labouring Classes in Early Industrial England 1750–1850*, Harlow, Longman.

RULE, J. (Ed) (1988) *British Trade Unionism 1750–1850: The Formative Years*, Harlow, Longman.

RUTHERFORD, A. (Ed) (1988) *Aboriginal Culture Today*, Kunapipi, Dangaroo Press.

SAAKANA, A.S. and PEARSE, A. (Eds) (1986) *Towards the Decolonization of the British Education System*, London, Frontline Journal.

SALTER, S. and STEVENSON, J. (Eds) (1990) *The Working Class and Politics in Europe and America 1929–1945*, Harlow, Longman.

SAMARA, A. (1989) *Palestine: Profile of an Occupation*, London, Zed Books.

SANDERS, D. (1985) *The Struggle for Health — Medicine and the Politics of Underdevelopment*, London, Macmillan.

SANDWELL DEPARTMENT OF EDUCATION (1987) *Britain and India: An Uncommon Journey*, Sandwell, Education Development Centre.

SARUP, M. (1978) *Marxism and Education*, London, Routledge and Kegan Paul.

SCHIROKAUER, C. (1991) *A Brief History of Chinese Civilization*, London, Harcourt Brace Jovanovich.

SCHOOLS COUNCIL (1976) *History 13–16 Project: What is History?*, Edinburgh, Holmes McDougall.

SEARL, C. (1989) *Grenada Morning: A Memoir of the 'Revo'*, London, Karia Press.

SEARLE, C. (1975) *Classrooms of Resistance*, London Writers and Readers Publishing Cooperative.

SEARLE, C. (Ed) (1984) *In Nobody's Backyard, Maurice Bishop's Speeches: 1979–1983*, (A Memorial Volume), London, Zed Books.

SEGAL, J.M. (1989) *Creating the Palestinian State: A Strategy for Peace*, Chicago, Lawrence Hill Books.

SELECT COMMITTEE ON RACE RELATIONS AND IMMIGRATION, (1969) *The Problems of Coloured School-Leavers (Parliamentary Papers Reports (1968–69) House of Commons 413 (Cmnd 19)*, London, HMSO.

SHAN, S. and BAILEY, P. (1991) *Multiple Factors: Classroom Mathematics for Equality and Justice*, Stoke-on-Trent, Trentham Books.

SIBANDA, M., MOYANA, H. and GUMBO, S.D. (1982) *The African Heritage*, Harare: Zimbabwe Educational Books.

SIU, B. (1981) *Women of China: Imperialism and Women's Resistance 1900–1949*, London, Zed Books.

SIVANANDAN, A. (1982) *A Different Hunger: Writings on Black Resistance*, London, Pluto Press.

SIVANANDAN, A. (1985) 'RAT and the degradation of black struggle', in *Race and Class*, **XXVI**, 4, London.

SIVANANDAN, A. (1989) 'New Circuits of Imperialism', in *Race and Class*, **XXVI**, 4, London.

SLACK, P. (1988) *Poverty and Policy in Tudor and Stuart England*, Harlow, Longman.

SPONG, J.S. (1989) *Living in Sin*, San Francisco, Harper Row.

STONE, M. (1981) *The Education of the Black Child: The Myth of Multiracial Education*, London, Fontana.

SUGARMAN, B. (1970) 'Social class, values and behaviour in schools', in CRAFT, M. (Ed) *Family, Class and Education*, London, Longman.

SZENTES, T. (1971) *The Political Economy of Underdevelopment*, Budapest, Akademia Kiade.

THAPAR, R. (1966) *A History of India: Vol. I*, London, Penguin Books.

THOMPSON, E.P. (1963) *The Making of the English Working Class*, Harmondsworth, Pelican.

TIERNEY, J. (Ed) (1982) *Race Migration and Schooling*, Eastbourne, Holt, Rinehart and Winston.

TIGER, L. and FOX, R. (1972) *The Imperial Animal*, London, Secker and Warburg.

TINKER, H. (1974) *A New System of Slavery: The Export of Indian Labourers Overseas 1830–1920*, London, Open University Press.

TOWNSEND, F. (1993) *The International Analysis of Poverty*, London, Harvester Wheatsheaf.

TREECE, H. (1962) *The Crusades: Two Hundred Years of War, Sacred Journeys and the Quest for Loot*, London, The Souvenir Press.

TROYNA, B. (Ed) (1987) *Racial Inequality in Education*, London, Tavistock Publications.

TROYNA, B. and CARRINGTON, B. (1990) *Education, Racism and Reform*, London, Routledge.

UNITED NATIONS (1992) *Human Development Report 1992*, Oxford, Oxford University Press.

References

VAUGHAN, M. (1991) *Curing Their Ills: Colonial Power and African Illness*, Cambridge, Polity Press.

VERMA, G.K. (Ed) (1989) *Education for All: A Landmark in Pluralism*, London, Falmer Press.

VERMA, G.K. and BAGLEY, C. (Eds) (1979) *Race Education and Identity*, London, Macmillan.

VILAR, P. (1969) *A History of Gold and Money 1450–1920*, London, Verso.

VINCENT, D. (1991) *Poor Citizens: The State and the Poor in Twentieth-Century Britain*, Harlow, Longman.

WA THIONG'O, N. (1983) *Barrel of a Pen*, London, New Beacon Books.

WALLACE, M. (1979) *Black Macho and the Myth of the Superwoman*, London, Platform Books.

WASSERSTEIN, B. (1991) *The British in Palestine: The Mandatory Government and the Arab-Jewish Conflict*, Oxford, Blackwell.

WATKINS, D. (1984) *The Exceptional Conflict: British Political Parties and the Arab-Israeli Confrontation*, London, Council for the Advancement of Arab-British Understanding.

WESTERGAARD, J. and RESLER, H. (1975) *Class in a Capitalist Society*, London, Heinemann.

WHITE, J. (1990) 'Black leadership in America', in Booker T. *Washington to Jesse Jackson*, Harlow, Longman, [Second edition].

WHITEHEAD, M. and DAHLGREN, G. (1991) *What can be done about inequalities in health?* The Lancet, Vol. 338: Oct 26, 1991, pp. 1059–1063.

WILLIAMS, E. (1934) *Capitalism and Slavery*, London, Bogle-L'Ouverture Publications.

WILLIAMS, E. (1970) *From Columbus to Castro: The History of the Caribbean 1492–1969*, London, Andre Deutsch.

WOMEN IN STRUGGLE (1978) London, Rising Free Bookshop.

WOMEN'S IMMIGRATION AND NATIONALITY GROUP (1985) *Worlds Apart: Women under Immigration and Nationality Law*, London, Pluto Press.

WOOD, W. and DOWNING, J. (1968) *Vicious Circle*, London, SPCK.

WORSLEY, P. (1984) *The Three Worlds: Culture and World Development*, London, Weidenfeld and Nicolson.

WRIGHT, A.W. (1983) *British Socialism 1884–1964*, Harlow, Longman.

WRIGHT, D.G. (1988) *Popular Radicalism: The Working-Class Experience 1780–1880*, Harlow, Longman.

ZINN, H. (1980) *A People's History of the United States*, Harlow, Longman.

Index

Printed in Great Britain
by Amazon

81243397R00106